THE
Healthy Eating
RECIPE BOOK

mothercare

THE
Healthy Eating
RECIPE BOOK

E L I S A B E T H   M O R S E

Conran Octopus

Contents

This book is dedicated to my sons, Christopher, who has learnt to eat almost anything that is put in front of him, and Matthew, who is still trying!

Art editor *Ann Burnham*
Editor *Diana Craig*
Editorial assistant
Dawn Sirrett
Photography
Julie Fisher
Food preparation
Valerie Barrett
Illustrations
Evie Safarewicz
Production
Sonya Sibbons

First published in 1990 by
Conran Octopus Limited
37 Shelton Street
London WC2 9PH
Text © 1990 Elisabeth Morse
ISBN 1 85029 295 7
Typeset by Litho Link Ltd,
Welshpool, Powys
Printed in Italy

Note The pronouns 'he' and 'she' have been used in alternating sections of the book to reflect that the text applies equally to male and female children.

Introduction

"What shall I give them to eat?" is a familiar question which most mothers ask themselves fairly frequently. The problem of finding foods which are reasonably healthy but which at the same time will be eaten by most members of the family can be a difficult one, and the recently highlighted problem of avoiding the risks of food poisoning is an extra complication.

Convenience foods

Feeding the family is a major preoccupation for parents and one which has to be coped with almost every single day — no wonder preparing meals can seem so tiring! To help cope with this problem 'convenience' has become a prime consideration in modern eating habits, whether it be in the form of pre-prepared foods, new speedier cooking equipment or large stores where all the shopping can be done and where a car is used as a glorified shopping basket.

'Convenience' has, however, resulted in many unforeseen consequences. Many hands may make light work, but mass-produced and preprepared foods are much more vulnerable to contamination because of the increased handling involved. Using convenience foods rather than cooking your own recipes means less awareness of the ingredients used so that an unhealthy balance of nutrients is much more likely. Modern preservatives may also have encouraged us to become a bit more slipshod about basic hygiene, so that when preservatives are removed from familiar items it is easy to forget that they may have to be stored differently. Buying foods on a weekly basis is only feasible if you have a large fridge, as a small one will not work efficiently if it is overloaded. Speedy cooking, such as that in a microwave, also requires learning different techniques from those which apply to conventional ovens.

Feeding the family healthily

Despite all these drawbacks, it is possible to feed the family healthily and safely without too much inconvenience, and this book is intended to show you how. The three principle aims of the book are: to give you a fund of meal ideas; to describe healthy methods of food preparation, using nutritionally desirable ingredients; and to offer a few basic guidelines on how to avoid children's common eating problems. Finding meals which everyone in the family will eat is not always easy, particularly when food likes and dislikes are a child's preferred method of expressing his or her individuality. Just as children's shapes and sizes can vary enormously, so can their appetites and the extent to which food seems of greater or lesser importance at the different stages in their lives.

Children and their stages of growth

For the first two years of life a baby's growth is mainly measured by weight. In the early months a child's growth is faster than it ever will be and by six months his or her birth weight has usually doubled. Growth slows down a bit in the next six months so that by the child's first birthday the birthweight will have tripled.

The toddler

After the first year, a child's weight gain slows noticeably and in the second year the average child only gains about 2.5 kg (5½ lb). From the age of two or three years, height takes over as the main indicator of a child's growth, though measuring weight is still important, particularly if a child is overweight. At three, a child's pot belly begins to disappear and the legs begin to lengthen.

The two-year-old The average two-year-old boy weighs 12.75 kg (28 lb) and is 86 cm (34½ in) tall. At the age of two, boys can normally weigh anything from 10.25 – 15.75 kg (22½ – 34½ lb), and be 80 – 92 cm (32 – 37 in) tall.

Girls at the age of two can weigh anything from 9.75 – 15 kg (21½ – 33 lb), and be 78.5 – 91 cm (31½ – 36½ in) tall. The average two-year-old girl weighs 12.5 kg (27½ lb) and is 85 cm (34 in) tall. ▽

The school-age child

Between the ages of five and ten a child's face changes, thinning out and lengthening as it gradually assumes adult proportions. It is not unusual for a child to be skinny at this age and for his or her ribs to stick out. Children of this age who are overweight through being overfed are usually also tall for their age. Differences in height between children of the same age become much more apparent during this period, though some of these differences may even out during puberty and adolescence when some small children will catch up with a big growth spurt and some tall children will stop growing sooner than others. Most children of this age take part in and enjoy plenty of physical activity. Because exercise is very important for health, their efforts need to be encouraged.

At around ten years, some children will also have started their pubescent growth spurt.

The five-year-old At the age of five the average boy is 108 cm (43 in) tall and weighs 18.5 kg (41 lb). The normal range for height is 99 – 117 cm (39 – 47 in) and the range for weight 14.5 – 23.5 kg (32 – 51 lb). ▽

Girls at five years of age are on average 107 cm (42 in) tall and weigh 18.5 kg (41 lb). The normal range in height is 98 – 116 cm (39 – 46 in) and for weight 14.5 – 23.5 kg (32 – 52 lb).

The ten-year-old At ten boys are on average 137 cm (55 in) tall and weigh 30.5 kg (67 lb). The normal range for height is 125 – 144 cm (50 – 57 in) and for weight 23 – 43.5 kg (50 – 95 lb).

At ten girls are on average 136 cm (54 in) tall and weigh 31 kg (68 lb). The normal range for height is 125 – 147 cm (50 – 59 in) and for weight 23 – 45 kg (50 – 99 lb). ▷

Avoiding eating problems

Healthy babies are born with an instinct to find food for themselves. The instinct of 'rooting' (searching) for the nipple is the first sign of this, as is crying when they are hungry and refusing to suck when they have had enough.

Letting children choose
In the beginning, a baby obviously needs someone else to supply the necessary milk, but from the age of 6 to 8 months, when babies are starting to sit up and reach out for things, many would be capable of starting the weaning process for themselves, simply by grabbing food from their mothers' plates. Here, the mother's role would be to make sure that suitable food lay within reach and that unsuitable or dangerous items were removed.

From 12 months, children discover that they themselves can decide which foods they will eat and they mainly show this by refusing what they do not want. As they get older, many children like to have an increasing say in what they are given and food fads or 'favourites' are common in about a quarter of all preschool-age children. They are also usually keen to 'help' with food preparation. Again this is all part of the natural process of seeking independence and learning to do things for themselves. By the age of five most children are quite capable of putting together a very simple cold meal, and by the age of ten of mastering some basic cooking skills — skills which they enjoy.

Growing independence
The urge to learn new skills is very strong in children and when thwarted it can be the commonest cause of eating problems. Babies may refuse to eat unless they can have a go at feeding themselves with a spoon or with their fingers; toddlers may develop fads as a way of having some say in what they are given to eat; school-age children will go into lengthy arguments about how their packed lunch should be like everyone else's; and teenagers may have very strong opinions about the sorts of foods they should be eating — which, as often as not, are a combination of very healthy and very unhealthy foods eaten at strange times. Recognizing that it is normal for a child to want to exercise some independence over what he or she eats is probably the key to managing the most common eating problems. These will not disappear overnight but by encouraging an atmosphere of trust you will be helping your children to develop more acceptable eating habits when they are ready.

Virtually all food problems can be grouped into two sorts: food refusal or a small appetite, and food fads. Similar methods of management apply to both.

Encouraging babies to feed themselves
Food refusal commonly starts at around a year old, although much younger babies may do this too. Babies under 6 to 8 months who refuse the spoon may simply not be ready to start weaning, whatever medical advice says! In such cases it is better to give up attempts at weaning for a couple of weeks and then gradually start again, or wait until he is able to dip a finger in some food and taste it for himself. In the meantime, breast or formula milk and vitamin drops will keep him healthy.

Babies who have taken to solids enthusiastically but then start refusing may simply be anxious to practise their hand skills rather than be spoon-fed. Here, a few small pieces of cooked vegetables and a spoon to hold will probably keep him occupied and happy while you spoon in the rest.

If your child is a toddler, the more you can let him make decisions for himself (which does not, of course, mean giving him an unlimited choice), the more he will feel like cooperating. It helps if you let him serve himself or at least point to what he wants from a serving dish. You will both get more satisfaction if he eats all of a very tiny helping rather than the same amount from a larger-sized portion.

A child can be encouraged to help with the shopping, to help think up ideas for meals and help with their preparation. Looking forward to other people's appreciation of his efforts in getting a meal ready is a first step in encouraging a positive approach to meals.

Learning sociable habits of eating
Growth slows down markedly in the second year and many babies are simply not as hungry. Activity is no indicator of appetite as some highly active children are simply very efficient users of a small amount of food energy. At this age toddlers may be much more interested in moving about and discovering their playing skills, so that sitting down to meals and eating tidily may be rebelled against. They have also yet to learn the adult habit of feeling hungry — or at least being able to eat — when the clock says it is time for a meal.

It is probably too much to expect an independent-minded young child to learn your family

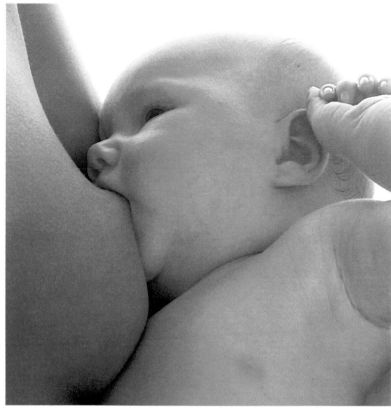

Left: *a baby enjoys the earliest experience of food and the comfort it brings*

participate in any discussions, particularly those that affect them. Talking about a toddler's eating problems in front of him is much more likely to strengthen his resolve to keep food a battle when he is going through the 'no' or negative stage. Older children may find such discussions painful reminders of their own earlier eating problems making it even harder for them to relax at mealtimes and enjoy food. During the toddler period, then, the best approach is to appear relaxed about eating and not to make an issue of it by talking about it a lot.

Once children start school their appetites generally increase and the worst of the eating problems are usually, but by no means always, over. Eating difficulties which persist after the age of five tend to take much longer to resolve, sometimes because both parent and child have grown used to the situation and have given up trying to do anything about it.

However, there is no reason why the methods used for managing younger children should not be modified and also used for older children. Remember, though, that the key is to negotiate a balance between their desire for independence and your experience of what is in their long-term interest.

During the school-age years coping with the pressure of what other children do or don't eat is a common bone of contention between parents and children. Talking about a problem and listening to each other's point of view not only encourages a healthy expression of feelings but also helps a child to mature.

eating habits all in one go, but you can tackle them one at a time. For example, you could start by making a rule either that all eating and drinking is done sitting down or that all between-meal snacks be of the bread, fruit or salad type.

Keeping mealtimes calm
A toddler is having to learn to cope with his own frustrations, like trying to get his clumsy hands to do what his brain wants them to do, so he may find it particularly hard to cope with his parents' frustrations as well when he refuses to hurry and eat something which he has no interest in. If mealtimes are emotionally highly charged it will help if you eat first, so that hunger does not affect your temper, and then let him eat

where he cannot see you but you can still keep an eye on him.

An older child can also find emotionally charged mealtimes difficult, so that sitting down for a meal depresses his appetite rather than stimulating it.

Eating between meals
If between-meal snacks are allowed, then at least make sure they are healthy foods (see page 74) rather than biscuits, crisps, sweets and sweetened drinks. Many children will determinedly forego nourishing food if there is a reasonable chance of their getting a favourite sweet or savoury snack instead.

Discussing, listening and negotiating
Although toddlers are not yet able to reason, they do like to

Healthy food

Healthy eating should be seen as something enjoyable and not merely a list of foods which should *not* be eaten. One of the commonest mistakes when trying to eat healthily is to cut down, or cut out, the so-called less healthy foods without finding something satisfying to replace them. Treating food in this way simply turns eating into a punishment rather than a pleasure. Instead it is better, at first, to eat more of those foods which you already eat which are good for you so that you have less room for the foods you wish to cut down on.

Next, you begin to experiment with less familiar foods, making those which you like an increasingly important part of your diet. Having a new baby is one of the commonest incentives for rethinking old eating habits and starting afresh.

Nutrition

Food is naturally made up of all sorts of chemicals, some of which we need and some which we could do without. Provided the body is given a reasonable variety of foods, it is generally quite efficient at sorting out what it needs and getting rid of what it does not. This system, however, is not fool-proof, and some people have constitutions which are better able to cope with excesses, deficiencies and poisons, whether they be those which naturally occur in foods or those with which food becomes contaminated. The body's natural ability to cope also changes with age: babies are much more vulnerable to food poisoning and growing children need more protein, vitamins and minerals than adults, whereas adults seem more vulnerable to excesses of items like fats and deficiencies of fibre.

Different groups of foods have various characteristics in common, and for this reason nutritionists usually recommend eating something from several different groups each day so that a variety of nutrients is eaten over the course of the day — or in the case of very fussy children over the course of several days!

Grains, seeds and nuts
This group consists of plant foods like rice, flour, oats, beans, peas and nuts. These foods are good sources of proteins (the protein mixture is even better when cereals and beans are eaten together as, for example, in beans on toast), vitamins, minerals, the few essential fats we need and fibre. Most of these foods are good sources of energy, mainly from carbohydrates and, except for most nuts, low in fat. In many cultures these foods have traditionally formed the bulk of

the diet. Unfortunately as nations get richer, people abandon these highly nutritious foods and eat more of the expensive luxuries or their cheaper imitations.

Poultry, fish, meat, milk and eggs
These foods are rich in proteins, vitamins, minerals and energy (from protein and fat), but contain negligible amounts of fibre or carbohydrate. Some also contain a lot of fat, some of which is useful (particularly that from oily fish), but most is undesirable. Fortunately lean or low-fat varieties of most of these foods are available.

A special word needs to be said about milk as far as children are concerned. Milk is both a good all-round food and a particularly good source of the mineral calcium, which is needed for growing bones. For this reason it is a valued food for young children, though if it is disliked, milk is not essential once a baby is fully weaned. However, if milk is still drunk, current medical advice is that it should be whole milk for the under-twos but can be semi-skimmed for those between two and five. Fully skimmed milk should only be given to older children. The reason for this advice is that many young children have small appetites and giving them skimmed milk (except in cooking) would be tantamount to putting them on an enforced slimming diet. A child who dislikes milk of any kind will usually make up the gap with other foods. If you are worried about a chubby toddler, as long as he is active, having a healthy diet and not eating sweets, biscuits or similar snack items, he should slim down of his own accord later on.

Fruits and vegetables
Most fruits and vegetables are good sources of vitamins, minerals and fibres. With the exception of avocados, bananas, potatoes and dried fruit, they are generally low in calories. The vitamins in these fruits and vegetables have a special role in protecting us from disease, including some of the common forms of cancer and heart disease.

Sugars, oils, fats, salt and other extracts
As a group, these foods have no protein, few vitamins and minerals and lack fibre. Although they are of little nutritional value on their own, they can be useful in improving the taste of healthier foods.

The problem with this group occurs when they are eaten to excess. For example, sugar is put to good use when it is used to sweeten sour fruit, but not when it is used to flavour water as in soft, fizzy drinks. Likewise, salt is a useful flavour enhancer, but it is only one of many herbs and spices and should be treated as such. Oils and fats have their uses in cooking and as spreads, but again we tend to eat too much of them nowadays. Instead of small amounts being used to flavour bland everyday foods, their use has been reversed — bread and chips are now cut thin to emphazise the taste of the butter or margarine and oil.

Right: the different food groups, arranged in bands according to their importance in the diet. At the bottom are the animal protein foods, such as eggs, fish, meat and dairy products; the band above is made up of fruit and vegetables, while at the top the widest band consists of grains, nuts and pulses, which should form the bulk of the diet. The narrowest band, down the left, includes those non-essentials, of low nutritional value, like sugars, fats and salt

Meal planning

At one time, the norm was for three square meals a day with no between-meal eating. Nowadays most adults report eating one main meal with four or five snacks a day. Families with young children tend to compromise and have two reasonable meals and a couple of lighter meals or snacks. The time at which these are eaten is really a matter of habit, practicality and personal preference.

Traditional eating patterns
In Western countries, we have tended to plan meals, particularly the main ones, according to the 'meat and two veg' principle. In such a meal the 'meat' (or fish or poultry) is the central ingredient with a fresh vegetable (or salad) and potatoes (or rice or pasta) tending to play a smaller role. This is in strong contrast to eating patterns in poorer countries where a single ingredient like a bowl of rice is the main item, with a few vegetables and perhaps some beans or, more occasionally, very small amounts of meat or fish (when they can be obtained) to lessen the monotony.

As we now know the eating habits of both 'rich' and 'poor' nations are not ideal. The poor have too little choice and the rich eat proportionately too many fatty and sugary foods.

Getting a better balance
There is, however, a middle course between the two types of diet. Research has shown that the healthiest diets seem to be those that resemble the traditional Mediterranean eating pattern. In this rice or pasta forms the main part of the dish, a vegetable sauce or a salad are the next biggest ingredient and finally meat, chicken or fish appear occasionally or play a relatively small part as one of several ingredients. This sort of pattern can be recognized in many other traditional cuisines. For example, Indian and Chinese cuisines may also have rice or noodles as the main ingredient with four or five smaller accompanying dishes, one or two of which may be meat, fish or a pulse like lentils.

When the balance of such meals is altered, so that the rice or pasta is eaten in much smaller quantities as a vegetable and then bulked out with a fattier item, they become much less healthy. Even so-called healthy salads can have their nutritional balance upset if the salad is dressed in an oily dressing, and there is little plain bread, potato or other low-fat food to 'offset' the dressing.

How much meat?
Meat, particularly if it is lean, is not actually harmful, but served in fair-sized quantities, as in the traditional 'meat and two veg' proportions, it can crowd out other good foods such as a greater variety of vegetables and the starchy foods with their important fibre and carbohydrate complex, as well as their own balance of vitamins and minerals. The one dish of the day where a starchy food is commonly the major ingredient is breakfast cereal served with milk (even better if a high-fibre, low-sugar cereal and a low-fat milk).

Vegetarian food
Making a more imaginative use of vegetables is something which can be learnt from vegetarian cuisines. Even children who do not like 'vegetables' will often eat them as sauces or in the form of soups. In these dishes, it is their flavour rather than their texture which is tasted.

The term 'vegetarian', however, should not always be thought of as synonymous with 'healthy'. Many vegetarian dishes rely too heavily on fatty ingredients like cheese, oils, pastry and eggs. Vegetarian dishes may not always be liked by confirmed meat-eaters but they can be made more acceptable if a little highly flavoured meat or fish, such as bacon or anchovy or even beef extract, is added to the dish.

Sample day's meals for a school child
Breakfast: Weetabix and milk, with peach slices, if liked
Packed lunch: ham and tomato sandwich, banana, fruit yogurt, low-fat, low-salt crisps, drink of water
Teatime: glass of fruit juice, rock bun, beans on toast (for those with large appetites)
Evening meal: Mince Roll (see page 59), mashed potato and green vegetable, fruit to follow, drink of water or milk

---

A healthy eating pattern
All in all, if you can aim for the following pattern of eating (see also pages 16-17) you should have a healthy diet which is high in fibre, low in fat and sugar and rich in protein, vitamins and minerals:
- fish and poultry three or more times a week
- lean red meat no more than two to four times a week
- one meal or a couple of snacks a day (besides breakfast) where bread, pasta, rice or potato or a similar food is the major ingredient
- six to eight servings of fruit and vegetables (including peas or beans occasionally) a day
- sugary foods and drinks at mealtimes only, rather than as replacements for healthier snacks

Storecupboard

Apart from knowing how to store foods safely, perhaps the most important habit to learn is to label any food stored in a cupboard or freezer with the date it was bought and/or the date it was first opened. These reminders will help you maintain a fresh supply of ingredients. This is particularly important in the case of items like dried pulses — where the beans can get too hard to cook properly after a few months — and flour products, which can go rancid. A large packet of sticky labels and a ballpoint pen always to hand is the easiest way of putting this aim into practice.

The following lists outline which foods to choose for your storecupboard, fridge or freezer.

Dairy products

This group consists of skimmed or semi-skimmed milk, or whole milk for very young children (see page 12); low- or medium-fat cheeses like cottage cheese, Ricotta, curd cheese, Mozzarella, Edam, Camembert or Brie (see 'General words of warning' opposite), low-fat Cheddar or hard, 'mature' cheeses, where the stronger taste enables a smaller quantity to go further; and low-fat yogurts, plain or with fruit but not colouring.

Fat and spreads

In this group are those margarines labelled 'high in polyunsaturates' or low-fat spreads (fine as long as you don't spread them twice as thick); and

soya, sunflower, corn, grapeseed, groundnut or olive oil (rich in unsaturate fats which can help replace items rich in unhealthy saturate fats, like butter or lard). Beware any oil labelled just 'vegetable' as it may be high in palm or coconut oil, (which is highly saturated).

Sauces, condiments and preserves

These are generally not needed in the diet for nutritional reasons, but are useful for adding flavour and interest to other foods. They include: reduced-sugar jams (store in the fridge); low-fat mayonnaise (bought in small quantities and, once opened, used within a few days); and lemon juice, herbs, spices, thinly

sliced celery and fresh spring onion for use, where appropriate, instead of salt in cooked dishes (cutting down salt is important for those at risk of high blood pressure as salt tends to aggravate this condition. Salt should never be added to baby foods).

Meats and fish
This group consists of lean cuts of meat (including liver and kidney), mince which is described as less than 10 per cent fat, and related meat products; any kind of fish; turkey (which is even leaner than chicken and is sold in various forms as mince, fillets, strips and escalopes); and low-fat sausages (you should sample different varieties as some are very salty).

Vegetables and fruit
This group includes any kind of vegetable or fruit, fresh or frozen; cans of chickpeas and kidney beans (less wasteful in cans if you do not often eat these pulses); and thick-cut oven chips (which are the least fatty kind of chips).

Cereal products
Cereal products include bread, flour, pasta, and rice, preferably wholemeal or brown (don't spurn white varieties if that is all that will be eaten, however, as they are still nourishing foods); wholegrain, low-sugar breakfast cereals; and wholemeal biscuits, crispbreads and fatless crackers.

General words of warning
Any food described as low-sugar, or low-salt or preservative-free is likely to need storing in the fridge unless it is dried, canned or frozen. No one should eat raw eggs or uncooked dishes using them; government medical advisers also currently recommend that pregnant women and babies under a year (and anyone else whose immune system is particularly vulnerable) should not eat cooked eggs either, except those in baked products. They should also avoid soft ripened cheeses like Camembert or Brie; bought, chilled cooked products like roast chicken portions; and ready-made salads. All these products have to go through many stages in their production and so are more prone to careless handling.

Planning and organizing

Shopping is one of those activities which, for many people, is less planned and more something which 'just happens' with experience. However it is worth taking a little time occasionally to think the whole business through and do some advance planning, especially if some change in your life means that your shopping habits also have to change.

Common reasons for changing shopping habits are: having a new baby and combining its daily walks with visits to the shops; having a child who wants to go vegetarian and so needs different meals; going back to work so that shopping is really only feasible once a week; and, most recently, wanting to shop in a more environmentally friendly way by, for example, avoiding goods with excessive packaging. Using these opportunities to rethink your shopping habits can save time and make shopping more of a pleasure, as well as making it easier for you to have on hand the right foods for the sort of diet you want to follow.

How often to shop

Making a list or several lists — the standby of so many people's lives — is still probably the best answer whatever your lifestyle. Having a 'master copy' of a regular list can help when it comes to reminding yourself of what you are likely to need.

If you can, it is worth doing one monthly shop for heavy bulky goods like toilet paper, cleaning materials, breakfast cereals, frozen, tinned and bottled goods, cartons of long-life milk and fruit juice, tea, coffee, jams, sugar, flour, rice, pasta and biscuits. Doing this will considerably lighten your load so that you then need to shop on a weekly basis only for such items as root vegetables, meat, yogurts, cheese, eggs, citrus and firm fruits. This can then be supplemented with very small purchases more frequently, on the way back from school or work, for more perishable items which need to be bought really fresh such as fish, bread, milk, soft fruit and leafy vegetables.

If it is really only practical to have one weekly shop, then it will help if you also do some meal planning. For example, meals on the first three days of the week will need to be made up from the more perishable items such as fresh fish and meat, leafy vegetables, mushrooms, soft fruit and speciality breads. For the last four days, you can rely on non-perishable items such as vegetarian meals based on grains and pulses; flans using frozen and root vegetables; frozen fish, baked potato, pasta and cheese dishes; and puddings such as crumbles made from uneaten soft fruit supplemented with stewed apples. Provided you also have an emergency supply of canned tuna, sardines, tinned tomatoes, frozen sweetcorn and a packet of sliced bread in the freezer, then you should still be able to give the children something in their packed lunch and for tea on the last day!

Where to shop

Supermarkets are undoubtedly the most popular place to shop and certainly offer the greatest variety of foods which are usually very fresh because their turnover is so high — but they have their disadvantages, too. Queues at the checkout can be tediously long; a car is essential if only as a 'shopping bag'; and many goods are excessively packaged. Some supermarkets also stock a range of organically grown foods. These are foods which are grown in an environmentally friendly way but which, ironically, tend to be highly packaged to retain their freshness. They can also be prohibitively expensive.

Local shops Buying food at local shops like the butcher, greengrocer and fishmonger has several advantages. Items are usually less heavily packaged, you can have a more personal service and you can get advice on how to prepare and cook less familiar foods. It is also easier to ask speciality traders to supply more unusual items, like wild game or exotic vegetables.

Health food shops Health food stores sell other things besides vitamin pills and herbal remedies. They are also places where food manufacturers often try out new and unusual lines such as salt-free

---

Reading labels

Wherever you shop, it is most important to read labels, particularly on the back of the package, for any special storage instructions and to check that the list of ingredients on the back corresponds with any claims on the front. For example, 'no added sugar' does not necessarily mean 'less sweet': it usually means 'no added sucrose'. Other sugars like glucose, fruit sugars and sweeteners may have been added instead. A label saying 'no artificial preservatives' will also probably mean that the food has to be stored in a fridge; and remember that ingredients have to be listed in their order of quantity, the biggest first.

Above: shopping for food can be a pleasant excursion that you can both enjoy

stock cubes, sugar-free snacks, fruit spreads, salt-free margarines, etc. Many familiar items such as wholemeal bread, brown rice and soya milk started life in health food shops before making it to the supermarkets. There are some drawbacks to health food shops, however. Be wary, for example, of chilled foods and fruits and vegetables sold in these small shops. Very often their turnover can be so small that such foods are not as fresh as they should be, so always ask the date when they entered

the shop as well as using your own judgment. You should also avoid buying items like nuts and beans from open sacks. They may look wholesome displayed in this way, but these conditions make them very vulnerable to infestation and mould.

Planning meals

Having a list of meal ideas can be very valuable when you are tired and lack inspiration, or for the times when you are going to be back late from work and partners or older children have to put

something together instead. In the latter case, a master file or book containing a few very simple ideas with instructions of what should be done and, if necessary, where the ingredients are kept, will enable others to help you better. It may also be a way of encouraging the rest of the family to take their share in making meals, so that the total burden of feeding the family does not rest with you.

Storing food

Fridge

The temperature in the middle of a fridge should be no more than 5°C. Check the temperature with a fridge thermometer after the fridge door has been kept closed for several hours. Because cold air drops, the top of the fridge will be warmer than the bottom — the temperature on the top shelf will be about 6°C and that on the bottom shelf 3-4°C. Logically, cooked food should be on the bottom shelf as most bacteria cannot grow at temperatures of 3°C or below. In practice, however, this is not always possible if you are having to store raw meat along with other foods. Raw meat should always be kept near the bottom to ensure that no contaminating juices drip on to foods which will not be cooked. Some fruits and vegetables do well in very cold but not freezing temperatures and others do better at slightly higher temperatures. Foods should not be crowded together: this not only prevents the fridge from maintaining a low enough temperature throughout but also makes cross-contamination of bacteria much more likely. The mechanical parts on the outside rear of the fridge also need to be cleaned regularly to remove dust or they may have difficulty circulating cold air around the food inside.

Freezer

The temperature should always be between -18° and -23°C. All foods should be labelled with what they are and the date they were put in the freezer. This is especially important if you have a large freezer that can hold a substantial quantity of bags, boxes and tubs: it is surprising how quickly you can forget what you have in your freezer, and when you put it in. Foods for the freezer should be well wrapped to prevent drying out and the possibility of contamination. They should be put into the freezer cold so as not to allow any nearby foods to accidentally thaw out for a short while. If any food does accidentally start to defrost it should be safe to refreeze (although the quality may be affected) *provided* ice crystals are still present. Ready-frozen food should be put into the home freezer within 1 hour of purchase. If items are stored for too long they tend to deteriorate in quality rather than become unsafe.

Storing dry foods

Once opened, dried foods like rice, flour and nuts should be stored in sealed or airtight containers, to keep out any invading insects as well as any damp or moisture. A little moisture and warmth turn floury foods into ideal culture grounds for moulds and other contaminants.

Bread is best kept unwrapped in a separate bin, such as the traditional enamel or earthenware container, or modern wooden or plastic box. Storing bread in a fridge, as opposed to a freezer, leads to it staling more quickly. Bread should also not be kept wrapped in plastic, unless made with preservatives, as it will sweat and so go mouldy quicker.

The list below gives the approximate length of time food can be stored in the fridge and indicates which foods to store on which shelf.

Storing food in the fridge

Top shelf: aubergines, courgettes, cucumbers, citrus fruit, melons, peppers, tomatoes. Eggs should preferably be kept in a box so as to guard against condensation which can wash bacteria through the shell into the egg; they should be used within 6 to 8 days.

Middle shelf: cooked meats (use within 2 to 3 days), contents of opened cans (empty into a dish and use within 2 days)

Bottom shelf: wrapped uncooked meat (use within 4 days), mince (use within 1 to 2 days), offal (use within 1 to 3 days), sausages (use within 3 days), fish (use within 1 to 2 days), poultry (use within 2 or 3 days), bacon (use within 7 days).

Salad compartment: apples, pears, berries, stone fruit, rhubarb, broccoli, cabbage, cauliflower, carrots, celery, leeks, lettuce, mushrooms, spring onions, sprouts, watercress (all in a polythene bag or cellophane wrapping to retain moisture).

Potatoes, garlic, onions, avocados, bananas and ginger should not be kept in the fridge as they are damaged by very cold temperatures. Bread also tends to stale quicker. These foods do best in a cool temperature. Potatoes also keep better in the dark.

Cold food should always be put into the fridge within 1½ hours of purchase. In very hot weather it is worth transporting frozen food home from the shops in an insulation bag.

Storage times

Apart from keeping cupboards clean it is important that food should not be stored for too long or else fat-containing foods may go rancid and dried foods may harden. To make sure of this, you could label containers with the date you filled them as a reminder.

- Use within 1 month of buying: shelled nuts
- Use within 2 months: savoury biscuits
- Use within 3 to 6 months: flour, unshelled nuts
- Use within 6 months: oils, breakfast cereals. Dried fruit and dried beans are best used within 6 months, though they will last a year in airtight containers
- Use within a year: rice, pasta, dried herbs and spices

Hygiene

To some extent adults can survive their own germs (whether other people can is a different matter), but babies have not yet acquired that degree of immunity. For this reason good hygiene is essential especially if there is a baby in the family. The dirtiest things in kitchens are people, pets, flies, vermin, dirty towels and dishcloths and raw food, especially meat which can easily ooze blood. The reason they are dirtiest is not only because they are natural bacteria traps but also because they are items which frequently come in contact with other items or surfaces which may be contaminated, so transferring germs from dirty places to clean areas. To prevent this cross-contamination, you should observe the following rules.

Wash hands frequently when in contact with food — before and after handling food, after touching pets, touching a skin spot or a cut, wiping noses, going to the lavatory, changing nappies, or emptying the rubbish bin. If you get into the habit of washing your hands every time you handle food, you will soon find that you do it automatically.

Keep tea towels, hand towels and dishcloths clean. Damp, warm fabrics with lots of crevices are ideal culture spots for any bacteria which get wiped up. Meat juices are best mopped up with kitchen paper.

Clean spills and food marks with detergent and hot water. Hot water evaporates quickly leaving crockery and work surfaces dry which also helps prevent the growth of bacteria.

Use separate chopping boards for raw and cooked meats. The crevices in wooden chopping boards can easily harbour germs so they need to be cleaned with particular care. Plastic-coated boards are better.

Always wash knives between use on different types of food. If all the food is to be cooked then the same knife can be used for them all, but if any item is to be served raw or has already been cooked then a clean knife is essential.

Wash vegetables in clean, cold running water. Washing vegetables in a bowl of water is likely only to transfer bacteria from one part of the vegetable to another rather than actually remove the germs.

Reheating foods

The following cooked foods are particularly good culture mediums for bacteria and these should be treated very carefully, only being reheated once or used up within a day or two.
- all cooked meats, meat products and poultry
- gravies, stocks and custards
- rice
- egg flans

Bacteria can multiply from a couple of hundred to several million in a few hours. In order to grow, bacteria need food, moisture, time and warmth. Most food-poisoning bacteria grow best between 5°C and 63°C. Thus food which needs to be kept chilled should be kept at around 3°C and food which is to be kept warm should be kept above 63°C. When reheating food, it should be allowed to get piping hot all the way through. Food which is to be refrigerated should be cooked, if necessary, then stored within 1½ hours of cooking. A food net over an uncovered casserole is useful during this cooling phase.

Useful equipment

Healthy eating depends not only on the right ingredients but also on having the right tools to preserve the nutritional content of the food, and to cut down on undesirable ingredients like fats.

Small blender
A small hand blender is useful for puréeing individual quantities of food, such as a baby's meal or a vegetable sauce. It is quick and convenient to use, and there is also less to wash up than there would be with a liquidizer.

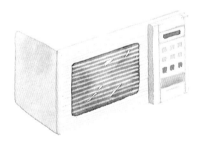

Microwave oven
Baked potatoes can be cooked in minutes in a microwave. Vegetables, including potatoes, retain much more colour and flavour (so avoiding the need for salt) and can be cooked and served in the same dish. In a microwave vegetables are cooked in a similar way to steaming. Fish is also excellent in a microwave, taking only a few minutes and creating no smell, very little mess and lots of flavour.

It is important to buy a microwave which can be controlled to cook to an exact number of minutes and seconds. A digitally controlled model with touch pads is more accurate than one with a manually controlled dial.

It is important to remember that microwaves do not sterilize and it is possible for food to have 'cold' spots which do not heat through evenly. For this reason it is important to follow instructions about stirring food during cooking and observing recommended standing times when the cooking process is continued.

Non-stick pans
A non-stick frying pan with a lid and a deep non-stick saucepan are invaluable for cooking with little or no fat. This method is called 'dry frying'. Dry-fried onions and other vegetables can be browned in only a teaspoon or two of fat; you can either heat a teaspoon or two of oil and then, when it is thin, let it run so as to oil the bottom of the pan, or you can pour in more fat and then pour off as much as possible when the oil has heated. A lid will help to soften the vegetables in their own steam.

Onions and meats can also be browned without any oil but they will need constant watching and stirring to prevent burning.

Steamer
Steaming is an alternative way of cooking vegetables, grains like rice and fish if you don't have a microwave. It helps retain vitamins and minerals and prevents overcooking. There are three types: the Chinese bamboo steamer, the fixed metal variety (where more than one steamer can be fitted on top of each other) and the Japanese collapsible type which will fit almost any pan.

Sharp knife
A sharp knife not only makes food preparation easier but is much better at helping retain vitamins in vegetables. A blunt knife crushes the plant cells releasing enzymes which destroy the vitamins. Used carefully, sharp knives should not be dangerous; they are most likely to cause cuts only when they are hidden by suds in washing-up water. Knives should always be stored in a safe place, out of reach of children.

First tastes

The key to successful weaning on to solids is, first, not to be in a hurry but to do it at your baby's pace, and, second, not to prevent him feeding himself if he is really keen to do so.

Babies can eat family food from the beginning, provided a few basic rules are followed. The rest of the family can enjoy 'baby foods', too. For example, vegetable purées, a traditional baby food, have a delicious fresh taste which can be enjoyed by every member of the family in soups, stews and as sauces for pasta. Fruit purées also make excellent, healthy toppings for puddings or are good mixed with yogurt. For the first 6 to 12 months of a baby's life, breast or formula milk is the main food and solids are an extra. Introducing new foods one at a time in the early weeks of weaning will enable you to detect any that don't agree with your baby.

recipes

Weaning

The best solid foods to start a baby on are fruit and vegetable purées and baby rice. These will provide him with extra vitamins and minerals and, in the case of a cereal like rice or a vegetable like peas, extra calories. Fruit and vegetable purées are usually well liked by babies as the puréeing process releases their natural sweetness so that they have a sweetish taste, reminiscent of breastmilk. Take care with salt, fats and sugar. Babies should never have salt added to their foods because their young kidneys cannot cope with it. They should also be given only small amounts of fat and added sugar as fats tend to be indigestible, and sugary foods and drinks are harmful to a baby's teeth.

Hygiene

Any equipment used in preparing baby foods must be scrupulously clean. Washing in clean, very hot, soapy water is adequate for bowls and spoons but extra care needs to be taken with blenders or sieves which have crevices which can trap food particles. If possible, stand these items in scalding water for five minutes before you use them.

Making purées

Unless you are puréeing some vegetables from a family meal it is often easier to prepare several batches of purée at once in order to freeze the surplus: for convenience, this can be done in ice-cube containers. (For information on freezing, see page 30). In order to make a smooth purée you will need to add some water (or cooking water in the case of vegetables which have been boiled). Meats in particular need plenty of liquid to help make them smooth so that they have the consistency of a thickish soup. If the mixture is too thick, a baby may gag; this may be more alarming for you than for him but may still put him off solids for a while.

Feeding your baby

Serve solids either cold or warm as you prefer but not hot. If you are reheating food, however, such as a defrosted portion, it should be reheated until piping hot and then allowed to cool to the right temperature.

recipes

BASIC STOCK

Vegetable stock is a reasonably quick stock to make and is an excellent way of using up many vegetable trimmings, provided they have been well washed and any bad bits removed.

To make the stock, always use carrot, potato, and some peppercorns (but omit salt). Then for a particularly good flavour, add any of the following: onion, celery (not too much as the flavour tends to be a bit overpowering), parsnip, leeks, fennel, tomatoes, apples, pears, garlic, and parsley stalks together with a bay leaf. You can also add broken cooked or washed uncooked bones (from which any fat or sauce has been removed).

Cut the vegetables and fruit into smallish pieces so that all the flavour can be extracted. Cover with water, bring to the boil, reduce the heat and simmer for ½ to 1 hour if you are using vegetables and/or fish bones, 2 to 3 hours if you are using meat or chicken bones.

Strain the stock and remove any fat when cold. Always taste the stock as occasionally it can be bitter if made with unsuitable vegetable trimmings.

Note Stock will keep for 3 to 4 days in the fridge or it can be frozen in 140 ml (¼ pint) quantities in ice cube containers. Store frozen blocks in a bag and use one or more when needed.

LEEK PURÉE

The puréeing process releases the natural sugar in leeks so that this purée tastes quite sweet.

450g (1lb) leeks, trimmed, washed and cut into 1cm (½ inch) lengths

Pour boiling water into a saucepan to a depth of about 1cm (½ inch). Add the leeks and cook until they are soft, in about 10 minutes.

Drain the leeks, reserving the cooking liquid. Purée the leeks in a blender and blend, adding sufficient cooking liquid to make a smooth purée. Add extra boiled water if necessary.

Variations Other vegetables, such as carrots or green beans, can be prepared in the same way. Potato should be sieved or puréed with plenty of milk, since on its own it can be glutinous and difficult for a baby to swallow.

PRUNE PURÉE

When babies first start solids they can often become a bit constipated — prunes are a useful antidote and have a pleasant, natural sweetness.

100g (3½oz) pitted prunes

Wash the fruit thoroughly to remove the mineral oils which are sometimes added to prevent sticking. Soak, if necessary, according to the instructions on the packet. (Some prunes are sold ready-prepared, and do not need to be soaked.)

Place the prunes in a saucepan and cover with fresh water. Bring to the boil, reduce the heat and simmer for 10 minutes, or until soft. Drain, reserving the cooking liquid.

Purée with some of the cooking liquid and sieve to remove any pieces of skin. Alternatively, rub through a sieve, adding sufficient cooking liquid to achieve the desired consistency.

This is easiest to do either by steaming or placing the food in a glass jar and steeping it in boiling water, giving it an occasional stir.

Begin by offering food at a feedtime when your baby has already had some milk and is not frantic with hunger. Let him suck a small amount off the tip of a spoon and give him the equivalent of one to two teaspoons at one feed in the first couple of weeks. Over the following weeks you can gradually build up the times and the quantities so that after a month or so he is having some solids three times a day. After another month, solids will probably have completely replaced one or even two breast or formula feeds depending on the age that weaning began.

Vitamin supplements
If, at any stage, your baby is not keen on fruits or vegetables you should give him vitamin drops. These are often advised as a precaution for all babies. Vitamin drops may also be necessary if your baby develops a dislike of breast or formula milk after starting solids. For the first year doctors recommend only breast or formula milk as these are richer in vitamins and minerals than ordinary cows' milk.

Above: the first solids, Leek Purée and Prune Purée

suitable first purées

VEGETABLES
carrots • cauliflower • leeks • broccoli • parsnips • swede • peas • lentils • green beans • thinned mashed potato

Avoid spinach until 6 months as it is high in oxalic acid which is difficult for a baby's kidneys to cope with. Sieve peas, pulses and tomatoes to remove the tough skins and seeds.

FRUITS
apples • pears • bananas • melon • peaches • apricots • stewed prunes

Either cook and purée the fruit, or mash the fresh fruit if very soft, or you can serve the fruit raw, very finely grated. Until your baby is 6 months old, you should avoid fruits with a lot of seeds like strawberries, raspberries, blackcurrants and citrus fruit.

MEAT
lean beef • chicken • very lean pork *or* lamb

Because of its texture, it is more difficult to achieve a smooth purée with meat than with vegetables or fruit. For this reason, it may be easier to leave meat purées of all kinds until later when your baby is well used to other solids and can cope with the new texture.

27

Foods from six months

At around 6 to 8 months, babies love to practise their growing skill at picking things up with their fingers and really enjoy this new experience. At this age, your baby will be able to take soft, well-mashed food and is also able to hold a rusk. From 7 to 8 months, she will be able to take a few soft lumps like cooked rice or small pasta pieces which can be added to purées to vary the texture. She will also be able to eat some breakfast cereals like porridge or wheat breakfast biscuits, soft sandwiches and pieces of banana or other soft fruit. Between 9 and 12 months your baby can start to have well-chopped meat and fish. Don't be alarmed if you find that your baby passes out lumps of undigested food into her nappies. This is perfectly normal and, provided she seems well, is not a cause for concern.

Eating such foods obviously depends on the ability to chew; this has little to do with the presence of teeth and more to do with the maturity of the jaw action. Being able to chew and bite begins at about 7 or 8 months, but is not well developed until 18 to 24 months.

Preferences

Some babies at this age show a definite preference for stronger-tasting adult dishes made with garlic, herbs, mild spices and even wine! (The alcohol has no effect as it evaporates during cooking.) Others prefer blander-tasting foods.

Foods to avoid

If there is a history of eczema, asthma or hay fever in the family then you may prefer to delay the introduction of particular foods which can trigger off such conditions. Doctors currently recommend that babies at risk of allergies have no wheat-based cereals before 8 months, no oranges or citrus drinks until 9 months and no dairy foods or fish until 10 months. If you are at all concerned about what your baby should or should not be allowed to eat, consult your doctor or health visitor.

Whole nuts are another food to avoid. They should never be given to children under five years because they can be inhaled or cause choking.

There has been much discussion over the safety of eggs, and who should or should not eat them. At the moment, doctors advise that all babies avoid eggs, whether they are raw or cooked (except those used in baking) because of the risk of contamination with the food-poisoning *Salmonella* bacteria.

recipes

LENTIL, OAT AND CHEESE BAKE

Unlike many other pulses, split red lentils do not need to be soaked before cooking, so they provide a convenient and tasty alternative to other vegetable dishes, and a change in texture.

Serves 4

170g (6oz) split red lentils
420ml (¾ pint) water
1 teaspoon oil
2 onions, peeled and chopped
4 heaped tablespoons porridge oats
2 stalks celery, thinly sliced
125g (4½oz) Edam cheese, grated
1 teaspoon mixed dried herbs
2 tablespoons tomato purée

Wash the lentils and place in a saucepan with the water. Bring to the boil, cover with a lid, reduce the heat and simmer for 15 to 20 minutes until soft and most of the water has been absorbed. Drain.

While the lentils are cooking, spoon the oil into a non-stick saucepan and heat until the oil runs easily over the base of the pan. Add the onions, stir and cover with a lid so that they soften in their own steam. Stir occasionally. Add the oats, celery, cheese and herbs to the onions in the pan, along with the drained lentils and the tomato purée.

Pour into a lightly greased shallow baking tin and bake in a preheated moderate oven, 180°C (350°F), Gas Mark 4, for about 30 minutes. This is soft when hot but becomes firm when cold. Cold leftovers are excellent with a salad.

LIVER CASSEROLE

Liver provides a wonderful gravy and is rich in iron. It should not be overcooked as overcooking will make it toughen.

Makes 2-3 baby portions

a few drops oil
¼ small onion, peeled and chopped
1 small piece lamb, calf *or* chicken liver, washed, dried and chopped in 2.5 cm (1 inch) pieces
½ tomato, *or* ½ teaspoon tomato purée diluted in a little water
extra water *or* milk as necessary (see Method)

Heat the oil in a non-stick frying pan, add the onion and allow to soften, stirring to prevent sticking. When the onion is soft, add the liver pieces to the pan and gently fry on all sides. Add the tomato, if used, and continue to cook gently. After 5 minutes, cut one piece of liver open to see how pink it is. Cook until the bright pink has faded to a pale pink, but do not allow it to go brown all the way through. If the liver starts to stick, add a little water to the pan.

When the liver is cooked, add enough water (with the tomato purée if you are using it) to dissolve any juices sticking to

recipes

the bottom of the pan, and simmer gently for another 3 to 4 minutes.

Remove from the heat, peel off the tomato skin and roughly purée the mixture, or mash, adding extra water or milk if the purée is too thick.

CHEESY POTATO
Serves 2
450g (1lb) potatoes,
peeled or scrubbed and thinly sliced
1 onion, peeled and sliced
140ml (¼ pint) milk

Below: Cheesy Potato served with grated raw carrot

freshly ground black pepper (optional)
60g (2oz) grated cheese

Place the potatoes, onion and milk in a saucepan. Bring to the boil, reduce the heat and simmer for 5 minutes. Season with pepper if you wish.

Pour the potato mixture into a lightly greased ovenproof dish, sprinkle the cheese on top and bake in a preheated, moderate oven, 180°C (350°F), Gas Mark 4, for 35 to 40 minutes.

Serve with a salad or raw vegetable sticks. This dish also makes a slightly

different accompaniment to fish dishes, or other low-fat family meals, instead of ordinary mashed potato.

SUITABLE FOODS
Cheese (chunks, grated, or cooked)
● yogurt ● ordinary milk
● liver ● fruits with seeds
like strawberries ● citrus fruit
● avocado ● spinach ● rhubarb
● pulses ● nut or sesame seed pastes
● fish ● custards made with cornflour
(but not egg)

Finger foods

From 6 or 7 months a baby is very keen to use his hands, picking up tiny objects like sweetcorn or peas, or exploring and splashing his food with his hands. Finger foods are a useful way of pacifying a very hungry baby who is waiting for his food as well as satisfying an urge to feed himself.

He may also have sore gums from teething at this age and some cold quarters of apple from the fridge or some pieces of frozen bread to bite on can be soothing. Large lumps of hard foods are safer than small pieces because a baby will grate or nibble off what he can manage, whereas he may choke on a small lump if it is put into his mouth whole. Trying to swallow large mouthfuls of soft food can also cause choking. Remember the rule: *whenever a child is eating he should always be closely supervised.*

Choking

If your child should choke on a hard object immediately put him over your knee face down with his head lowered; give him four sharp slaps between the shoulder blades to dislodge the object; finally scoop out the item from his mouth with your finger.

Freezing and storing

If you are eating the same meal as your baby but at a different time you should ideally cook fresh for

him and reheat the dish for yourselves. If you do reheat food for a baby, it should be no more than 24 hours old and have been stored properly in a fridge.

On the other hand, if you plan to cook in bulk for a baby, the food will be 'fresher' if you freeze it as soon as possible. Clean yogurt pots, ice cube trays and margarine tubs are very useful freezer containers, covered with lids, foil or stored in a strong polythene bag.

The golden rules for freezing are: allow food to cool as quickly as possible after cooking; once cold, and no more than 1½ hours after cooking, put the food in the fridge to get really cold for up to an hour, then put in the freezer; cover the food to prevent dehydration; label everything clearly with the contents and date of preparation.

Reheating frozen meals

Either allow the food to thaw in the fridge for a few hours so that it is kept below 5°C and then

reheat until it is piping hot *or* loosen the contents of a container by holding the outside under cold running water and then cook in a saucepan with a little stock or water, or place in a bowl and steam in a steamer.

Right: a selection of finger foods

Meal suggestions
Breakfast: cereal and milk; wholemeal bread or toast with a scraping of polyunsaturate margarine; piece of fruit; drink of breast or formula milk
Midday: finely minced meat or cheese with vegetables; rice pudding or yogurt and stewed fruit or ripe pear; water
Late afternoon: banana or sardine sandwich or pizza squares; rusk and fruit juice

Babies under 12 months will probably want an extra milk feed at the beginning or end of the day.

---

recipes

HOME-BAKED RUSKS

These have a pleasantly nutty, melba-toast-type flavour and are excellent for nibbling and sucking. They will keep for a couple of weeks in an airtight tin.

Makes 12
4 slices wholemeal bread,
1cm (½ inch) thick, crusts removed
Cut the slices of bread into 4cm (1½ inch) wide fingers and bake in a preheated cool oven, 150°C (300°F), Gas Mark 2, for 30 minutes.
Variation You could cut the bread into fancy shapes, but beware of using any with sharp points (like the arms and legs of gingerbread men) as these could hurt your baby's mouth, or break off too easily inside the mouth.

SUITABLE FINGER FOODS

Try the following finger foods:
banana chunks ● apple, peeled, cored and quartered ● pear, peeled, cored and quartered ● peach, peeled and quartered ● melon chunks ● fingers of tender cooked meat ● fish fingers ● fingers of pizza ● bread sticks, broken into 5 cm (2 inch) lengths ● sandwich soldiers ● bread soldiers ● cooked peas or sweetcorn kernels ● cooked sticks of carrot, cauliflower, broccoli, green bean, or lightly cooked courgette, parsnip, swede ● cooked potato ● grated raw carrot ● cooked chickpeas or other beans ● cooked pasta shapes ● cooked grains of rice ● small slices cheese

---

Food values: **RUSKS AND BISCUITS**	
	sugar
rusk, plain	4g
rusk, low-sugar	3g
rusk, wholemeal	3g
plain semi-sweet biscuit	2.25g
cream cracker	0g
rye crispbread	.5g
½ slice toast	.5g

Breakfast

Common sense suggests that something to eat early on in the day is a good idea, and that hunger makes for tired, irritable children who cannot concentrate fully on school work. However, breakfast is probably really only essential for those who are used to having it regularly; for such people going without breakfast can be very upsetting. From the nutritional point of view, breakfast is a useful meal for quite a different reason: it provides an opportunity to eat good-sized portions of fibre-rich foods like breakfast cereals and wholemeal bread.

A child who is hungry at the start of the day may want a large breakfast, and this may be cooked or may simply be two or three large bowls of cereal. As with all meals, try to encourage the eating of some fresh fruit or vegetables, such as a grilled tomato, fruit juice, or fresh or stewed fruit.

recipes

Continental breakfasts

Many people can only face a very light snack at breakfast, but children may benefit from being encouraged to eat a bit more at this time of day. One of the best ways of encouraging appetite is to have a bit of variety. Instead of plain toast, for example, you could try bagels, heated in the microwave or in the oven, croissants, brioche or sweet chola bread, all of which have the advantage of tasting good without the addition of any butter, margarine or jam.

The benefits of bread
Bread is one of the foods we should all be eating more of,

especially if it is thickly cut and only lightly spread with fat, and you can, of course, make your own, preferably wholemeal, bread. Bread recipes usually include salt, but this is not always necessary particularly if another flavouring agent like treacle or molasses is added. Not adding salt will also help the dough to rise a bit quicker. Homemade wholemeal bread is good toasted, and is an excellent source of fibre.

Jams and spreads
Next best to the taste of wholemeal toast is what goes on it. You can buy sugar-reduced jams, such as blackcurrant, in

which some Vitamin C manages to survive the jam-making process, unlike other fruits. You could also make your own marmalade, or fruit conserve or curd. These, unlike jam, provide fibre, minerals and far less sugar. Make them in small quantities and they will keep for a few days in the fridge.

If you prefer savoury spreads like yeast extract, remember that they have a high salt content so should not be given to babies. For small children or anyone at risk of high blood pressure, spread it very thin.

Many children are much more adventurous than adults about

Below: Hedgehog rolls, Fruit Spread, Fruit Curd, Scandinavian Start

the sorts of foods they will eat at breakfast, so another type of breakfast to offer is the Scandinavian variety where cold meats and cheese accompany the bread or rolls.

Whatever kind of breakfast you plan, try to make it follow a pattern of healthy eating so that it includes some cereal or similar food, some fruit or vegetable, and a bit of high-protein food like milk, beans, cheese or meat. Toast and fruit juice goes part of the way towards this, but adding a yogurt or a milky drink would improve the balance of the meal. Other options could be hot chocolate with French bread and a piece of fruit, or fruit spread or cheese on thick toast with a glass of fruit juice.

Food values: **BREADS**		
	protein	fibre
wholemeal, 1 slice	2.5g	2.5g
brown, 1 slice	2.5g	1.5g
white, 1 slice	2.25g	.75g
granary, 1 slice	2.75g	2g
white roll, 1	6.5g	1.75g
brown roll, 1	6.5g	3g
croissant, 1	4.75g	1.5g

recipes

WHOLEMEAL BREAD AND ROLLS

Breadmaking is not difficult: here is a quick bread recipe. Make sure the yeast you use is not too old: if it is, it will not froth up and make the dough rise.

Makes 1 × 1kg (2lb) loaf
110ml (4fl oz) boiling water
220ml (8fl oz) cold water
1 tablespoon molasses or black treacle
or **1 teaspoon sugar**
2 × 5ml teaspoons dried yeast
450g (1lb) wholemeal flour
½-1 teaspoon salt (optional)

Tip the flour into a bowl and place in a cool oven while you prepare the yeast: warming the flour and the bowl will help the yeast to work.

Meanwhile, in a warmed jug, dissolve the molasses, treacle or sugar in a quarter of the hot water. Leave to cool a little, until warm. Add the yeast, stir and leave for 10 minutes until frothy.

Mix the flour with the salt, if you are using it, in a large bowl. Make a well in the centre, pour in the yeast mixture and mix with a spoon, gradually adding the rest of the water. The dough should be soft and floppy. If there is too much flour add a little extra warm water or a little more flour if the dough is too sticky. Mix and knead with your hands until no trace of dough or flour is left in the bowl.

Shape the dough into a loaf and place in a well-oiled 1kg (2lb) loaf tin.

Generously dust the top of the loaf with flour and cover with a damp cloth. Leave to rise in a warm place for about 30 to 45 minutes, or until the dough almost reaches the top of the tin.

Bake in a moderately hot oven, 200°C (400°F), Gas Mark 6, for 45 minutes. You can check to see if the loaf is cooked by turning out and tapping the bottom: it should sound hollow.

Leave to cool on a wire tray, loosely covered in a cloth if you want the bread to have a softer crust.

Variation To make rolls, allow the dough to rise in a well-oiled saucepan, covering it with a lid. (If you prefer a softer dough, use half milk and half water, and half wholemeal and half white flour.)

Divide the dough into six, knead and shape into rolls. Place on an oiled baking tray and bake as above for 20 to 25 minutes. Wrap in a tea towel to prevent the crust from getting too hard, and cool on a wire rack.

To make 'hedgehog' rolls *as in the photograph, shape the dough into a round, divide into 6 triangles, rounding each into a hedgehog shape. With scissors, snip and raise the dough to form prickles. Punch holes for the eyes with the handle of a wooden spoon.*

SCANDINAVIAN START

Serves 1
1 to 2 slices Edam *or* **similar cheese**
1 slice ham *or* **tongue**
hot roll *or* **slice fresh bread**
raw vegetables, cut into sticks

Arrange all the ingredients on a plate, in whatever way you like, and serve.

FRUIT SPREAD

Although fresh fruit can be used for this, dried fruits produce a thicker, sweeter, more spreadable result. Other fruit, such as apricots, apples, pears and prunes can be used instead of peaches.

Makes 140ml (5fl oz)
100g (3½oz) dried peaches *or* **other dried fruit, as above**
water to cover

Place the peaches in a mixing bowl, cover with the water and soak according to the instructions on the packet. Turn into a saucepan, bring to the boil, reduce the heat and simmer until the peaches are soft, about 20 minutes.

Purée or rub through a sieve, and refrigerate. This will last for a few days in the fridge — if not eaten up before!

Note This spread is excellent for making your own fruit yogurts.

FRUIT CURD

Mixing peach purée (see previous recipe) with *fromage frais* or curd cheese makes a delicious spread. Curd cheese makes a thicker, firmer mixture, while *fromage frais* gives a softer fruit curd, with a slightly creamier taste rather like peaches and cream. These fruit curds are much less sugary and fatty than traditional jam and butter.

Makes 120ml (4fl oz)
60g (2 oz) fruit spread
60g (2 oz) curd cheese *or* **fromage frais**

Mix well and chill. Spread the curd straight on to toast or bread.

Cereals and fruit

A bowl of wholegrain breakfast cereal at the start of the day is one of the easiest ways of getting fibre into your diet. Wholewheat also has important vitamins and minerals as well as complex carbohydrates — a healthier source of energy than fats.

Fibre
There are several sorts of fibre in food: insoluble fibres, found in wholewheat, which are good for the digestive system; and soluble fibres, found in fruit and oats, which are good for the blood. An adult is recommended to have 30 grams (about an ounce) of fibre a day — half as much again as what is normally eaten. Two wheat breakfast biscuits and one slice of wholemeal toast provide almost a third of the adult recommended amount.

Eating bran on its own may improve the health of your bowels but it will not provide all the other nutritional advantages that cereals provide, so it should only be used as a temporary measure or as part of prescribed medical treatment.

Fruit provides both sweetness and fibre. Fruit fibre is commonly known as pectin, which is a natural gelling agent.

Sugar
Sugar is one of those foods which is of very limited value. Not only does it provide no fibre, but it does not contain any vitamins, minerals or protein either. It is also bad for the teeth.

It is sensible to start children off on cereals without sugar. However, if having sugar on breakfast cereals is the only way your child will eat them, you will have to judge whether the sugar is 'worth it'.

recipes

HOMEMADE YOGURT
Homemade yogurt tastes a bit milder than shop-bought yogurt and is more acceptable to young children. It will keep in the fridge for up to 10 days.

Makes 1 litre (1¾ pints)
1 litre (1¾ pints) long-life skimmed milk
1 heaped tablespoon dried skimmed milk
1 teaspoon plain low-fat yogurt

Pour the milk into a saucepan and heat until it is hot but not boiling or it will burn. (If you use fresh milk, it must reach boiling point to kill off any bacteria.) Meanwhile scald a mixing bowl (and a 1 litre/1¾ pint thermos flask if you are using one) with boiling water; this will ensure that the only bacteria you culture are the ones from the yogurt, and that the containers are warm enough to activate the milk culture when it is added.

Stir the dried milk into the hot liquid milk. The dried milk enriches the flavour and gives the bacteria extra nutrients to feed on. Leave to cool until the temperature reaches 47°C. If you do not have a cooking thermometer, test with your little finger: it should be able to stay in the hot milk for five seconds.

Place the yogurt in the bowl and mix in a little of the milk, then add the remaining milk and stir. Either pour into a warmed thermos flask and seal for 5 to 6 hours, or cover the bowl with cling film, wrap in a thick towel or tea cosy and place in a warm, draught-free place such as an airing cupboard overnight.

Once the yogurt is set, refrigerate. This yogurt can be used as the culture for successive batches over several weeks.

CEREAL BOX MUESLI
Children can get a lot of pleasure from making their own 'muesli'. It can also be a useful way of using up the irritating crushed leftovers of cereal at the bottom of the packet. The following is a good combination but the best is one made by the person who is going to eat it!

Serves 2 to 3
1 Weetabix *or* 1 Shredded Wheat
1 tablespoon each Shreddies and branflakes
2 tablespoons porridge oats
½ tablespoon crushed flaked almonds *or* dessicated coconut
½ tablespoon raisins *or* other dried fruit

Mix all the ingredients together. Serve with milk or fruit juice and some sliced banana, ripe pear or stewed fruit on top.

PANCAKES WITH FRUIT FILLING
Makes 8 pancakes
Batter
110g (4oz) wholemeal flour
1 egg
275ml (½ pint) milk
2 teaspoons oil
Filling
1-2 tablespoons fruit purée, such as apple, *or* mashed bananas, for each pancake

Make the pancakes. Either blend all the ingredients together in a processor, or beat the flour into the egg a little at a time, adding sufficient milk to keep the mixture soft. Add the remaining milk and oil, and beat the batter to make sure it is thoroughly mixed and free of lumps. Allow to stand for 10 minutes.

Heat a few drops of oil in a non-stick pan and, when it is beginning to smoke, brush the oil round the pan with a piece of paper to prevent sticking.

Pour sufficient batter into the pan to make a thin circle. Cook over a medium heat for about a minute. When the mixture is set, or the edges are curling slightly, turn the pancake over and cook the second side. Place the hot pancakes between two plates. Keep in the oven or over a pan of hot water.

Food values: CEREALS, MILKS AND YOGURTS		
cereals: 1 bowl	sugar	fibre
Coco Pops	7.5g	0g
cornflakes	2g	1g
Weetabix (2)	2.5g	5g
Shredded Wheat (2)	0g	5.5g
milks & yogurts	fat	sugar
skimmed milk, 1 glass	.25g	8.5g
semi-skimmed milk, 1 glass	2.75g	8.5g
full-cream milk, 1 glass	6.5g	8g
low-fat plain yogurt, 140g (5oz)	1.5g	9.5g
fruit yogurt, 140g (5oz)	1.5g	27g
Greek yogurt, 140g (5oz)	6-12.5g	3-8g

Right: Cereal Box Muesli

Place a tablespoon of fruit along one edge of each pancake, roll up, and serve. *Note Any surplus pancakes can be kept in the fridge for a couple of days or can be layered on greaseproof paper and frozen. To reheat simply place the pancake in a hot, ungreased non-stick frying pan for 1 to 1½ minutes (frozen pancakes take half a minute longer).*

BANANA AND ORANGE FLOAT
Serves 1
⅔ glass orange juice
½ banana
Place ingredients in a blender and whizz up for a thick and light milk-free 'shake'.

MILK SHAKE
A child who does not want to eat may be persuaded to drink a milk shake, especially if he or she has made it!
Serves 1
⅔ glass of milk
½ mashed banana *or* 2 tablespoons mashed strawberries *or* 2 teaspoons drinking chocolate (dissolved in hot water if necessary) *or* 1 tablespoon blackcurrant cordial *or* 1 tablespoon prune *or* other fruit purée
Place the milk and flavouring in a blender, whizz until frothy and serve.

Cooked breakfasts

Breakfast does not have to be hot in order to be nourishing, but some people do prefer cooked foods to start the day. Healthy, cooked breakfasts include: porridge; tomatoes or mushrooms on toast; baked beans; and smoked fish.

Taking care with eggs

There is no way of guaranteeing any egg to be *Salmonella*-free. However, dirty or cracked eggs should be avoided because bacteria can easily have entered from outside. Raw eggs should not be eaten by anybody, whatever their age, so drinks like egg nogs and flips cannot be recommended. On the other hand, tests have shown that well-cooked scrambled eggs and omelettes do reach a high enough temperature to be 'safe'. Soft-boiled eggs and eggs fried on one side do not reach a high enough temperature, though they may only present a risk to pregnant women, the very young, the very old and the sick.

Grilling or frying?

Nutritionists argue that grilling is preferable to frying because it allows fat to escape and run off foods like bacon and sausages, whereas frying creates an additional layer of fat on the food. However, this is not true of dry-frying methods in a non-stick pan, where only a little fat is used. Dry-frying, like grilling, encourages fat to run out of foods like bacon and sausages and, using this method, even bread can be fried in no more fat than would be used to spread on a piece of toast.

Food values: COOKED BREAKFAST DISHES		
eggs	protein	fat
boiled	7g	6g
fried	7g	10g
dry-fried (see Motorway Start)	7g	7g
scrambled (with knob of fat and whole milk)	7g	15g
poached (with knob of fat)	7g	8g
bacon		
1 back rasher, grilled	7.5g	10g
2 streaky rashers, grilled	7g	11g
sausages		
2 small grilled or fried	5.5g	10g
bread (1 whole slice)		
fried in fat	2.5g	14g
dry-fried	2.5g	5g
toast, lightly spread with butter or margarine	2.5g	5g
baked beans		
110g (4oz)	6g	.5g
pancakes		
1 thin	4g	3-16g

recipes

MOTORWAY START

Some children like a cooked breakfast. The traditional, fried breakfast is excessively fatty, however, so here is a less fatty, more healthy alternative.

Serves 1
Oil, for brushing pan
1 rasher lean bacon, with rind removed
½ slice bread
1 cold cooked potato, sliced
1 egg
Garnish
1 tomato
1 lettuce leaf

Brush a non-stick frying pan with a little oil and heat until the tiny droplets run easily. Add the bread and the potato and cook until toasted, turning over 2 or 3 times to prevent sticking. Remove the bread and potato and keep warm.

Add the bacon and tomato to the pan and when a little fat has run off the bacon, turn over and add the egg. If the bacon provides no fat, brush a small area of the pan with a little extra oil before adding the egg.

Serve when cooked as firmly as liked. Garnish with tomato and lettuce.

COWBOY MUNCH

This idea came from a book about cowboys. Real cowboys also had fresh baked biscuits, but Oat Crunchies (page 78) make a delicious substitute.

Serves 1
oil, for brushing pan (see Method)
1 pancake, made with 3 tablespoons batter (see page 36)
baked beans
1 glass orange juice

If you are using a pancake which has been previously cooked, or frozen, reheat it in a hot, ungreased non-stick frying pan, for 1½ minutes (frozen pancakes will take half a minute longer).

Place the beans in a saucepan and heat. Roll up the pancake and arrange on a serving dish with the beans. Serve with a glass of orange juice.

PIPERADE

Serves 1
1 teaspoon oil
½ small onion, peeled and finely chopped
¼ red pepper, chopped
½ clove garlic, crushed
1 tomato, chopped
1 egg, beaten
fresh ground pepper
chopped parsley, to garnish (optional)
toast spread with herb-flavoured butter, to serve

Pour the oil into a non-stick frying pan and heat until it runs easily over the base. Add the onion, pepper and garlic, and stir. Cover with a lid and allow to soften.

Add the tomato and cook for a further minute, then add the egg and stir while cooking. Season with pepper, garnish with parsley, and serve with toast.

recipes

BLT

A BLT — bacon, lettuce and tomato sandwich — makes a delicious and different savoury breakfast which is very easy and quick to prepare.

Serves 1

2 slices bread
1 lettuce leaf
4 slices tomato
1 or 2 rashers lean bacon,
such as back

Cut the rind and fat off the bacon. Either cook the bacon under the grill or in a non-stick pan, without any added fat, turning it over a couple of times to prevent it sticking to the pan.

Remove the bacon, cut in half and lay on one piece of bread. Top with the tomato, lettuce and second piece of bread. Press the bread down firmly, cut the sandwich in half and serve immediately while still warm.

PORRIDGE TOPPERS

Oats are a healthy source of fibre and a warming start to the day: they make a very satisfying breakfast, especially in winter. Although rolled whole oats have a grainier texture than quick-cooking oats, there is very little difference in the fibre content. Various toppings can be added to make the traditional bowl of porridge a bit more interesting.

Make up the porridge according to the instructions on the packet. Pour into bowls and serve with a little cold milk, poured around the edge, to cool it.

Eat the porridge as it is or top with a fruit purée, stewed prunes or mashed banana. Less healthy but rather nice is a little brown sugar sprinkled over the surface or a drizzle of golden syrup.

Below: Motorway Start

Packed meals

Children love picnics — they love sitting on the ground with a cloth spread in front of them, they love the freedom of eating with their fingers, they love the informality of eating outside and they love the excitement of opening a food parcel like a bag or a lunch box — even when they know the contents! In fact, knowing what they are going to find is one of the charms as far as children are concerned — but one of the worries for parents who might like to introduce new and more varied foods to their children, particularly when packed lunches are an everyday occurrence rather than an occasional treat. It is important for your child to understand that there is a difference between the daily packed lunch, which is a meal, and the special picnic, where more 'treat' foods may be served.

recipes

Sandwiches

Packed lunches are preferred to school dinners by many children and parents but they can have their drawbacks, the main one being lack of variety. In one survey of packed lunches the typical contents were a packet of crisps, a cheese or ham sandwich, a chocolate biscuit and an apple (which frequently ended up in the bin!). This sort of lunch is not only short on fruit and vegetables and quite fatty but, eaten day after day, it does little to encourage more adventurous eating. A few simple measures, which need not involve a lot of effort, could do a lot to improve such a meal. For example, using low-fat, low-salt crisps, and a low-fat cheese like Edam, and 'buttering' only one slice of bread in a sandwich would reduce the fat content; putting in some carrot sticks and cucumber chunks, together with a quartered orange, a couple of plain digestive biscuits and a carton of milk shake — would add healthy variety and interest.

Sandwiches are the traditional lunch box food, and although it may not seem very imaginative to provide them day after day, they do have one big advantage: they are an excellent way of encouraging the consumption of more bread, particularly if the bread is cut thick or served as chunky rolls or baps. Although wholemeal bread is rich in fibre and nutrients, white bread is nourishing too. There is a wide range of breads in the shops and it is possible to find wholemeal bread which is almost as soft and light as white bread as well as white breads which are fibre and nutrient enriched. Encouraging a liking for a variety of breads is good for the tastebuds, particularly if a child likes only a few sandwich fillings.

recipes

CHICKEN LIVER PÂTÉ

This is a soft pâté and best the day after it is made. Keep refrigerated and use within 2 days of making.

Makes 225g (8 oz)

225g (8 oz) chicken livers
2 *or* 3 good-sized sprigs of parsley (leaves only)
50 ml (3½ tablespoons) orange *or* tomato juice
1 medium onion, peeled and chopped
a little stock *or* water with a dessertspoon of lemon juice added

Place the livers and parsley in a mixing bowl, and pour over the orange or tomato juice. Place the onion and garlic in a small heavy-bottomed saucepan, and add the stock or water and lemon juice. Bring to the boil, reduce the heat and simmer until the onion is tender, stirring to prevent sticking.

Add the liver mixture, bring to simmering point again and cook for about 10 minutes, or until the outsides of the livers are just browned and the insides are still pink (overcooking will make the liver tough, dry and bitter).

Drain off the cooking liquid and reserve. Blend the liver in a food processor, with about half the reserved cooking liquid, until smooth (or mash thoroughly). Chill before using.

SMOKED MACKEREL PÂTÉ

Serves 225g (8 oz)

110g (4 oz) smoked mackerel fillet
1 small onion, finely chopped
½ teaspoon creamed horseradish *or* paprika pepper (optional)
1 teaspoon lemon juice
110g (4 oz) curd cheese *or* plain fromage frais

Place the fish, onion and flavourings in a food processor, and process lightly, or the mixture may end up too liquid. Alternatively, mash thoroughly with a fork. Stir in the cheese until well blended. Chill before using.

MAYONNAISE AND YOGURT DRESSING

Some fillings like chopped chicken and egg need something to bind them together so that the contents do not fall out of the sandwich. Using this light, tasty dressing can also mean less margarine or butter on the bread.

Makes 140g (5 oz)

70g (2½ oz) low-fat mayonnaise
70g (2½ oz) low-fat plain yogurt, *or* a little more if required (see Method)

Place the mayonnaise and yogurt in a mixing bowl, and whisk together. You may need to add a little more yogurt if you think the mixture is too thick.

Variations To make a thousand-island-type dressing, add a dash or two of tomato ketchup, to taste.

To make aioli, stir in a clove or two of crushed garlic. This is also good with barbecued meats.

SUGGESTIONS FOR SANDWICH FILLINGS

Sandwiches are healthy foods but are made even better if butter or margarine is used sparingly — it is not always necessary to use it anyway if the filling is moist. In the case of fattier fillings (see the 'food values' box), leaving out the butter or margarine altogether would considerably improve the nutritional balance of the sandwich.

Here are some suggested fillings: turkey with coleslaw • grated cheese mixed with grated carrot • tunafish mixed with diced peppers, cucumber, sweetcorn and mayonnaise • cottage cheese and banana • peanut butter and grapes • Fruit Curd (see page 35) • hummus and spring onion • egg (hard-boiled for at least 7 minutes), tomato and red pepper • *fromage frais or* curd cheese with diced peaches • cream cheese with pineapple • mashed avocado, mixed with a little lemon juice to prevent browning, and prawns

Food Safety

Although sandwiches will normally still be safe to eat after a few hours in a lunch box, there could be problems in very hot weather, depending on the sandwich filling used. Sandwich fillings which are the least risky are those with some kind of preservative such as salt in them. To be on the safe side, you could put in a picnic ice pack (supplied for cool boxes) which will at least keep the contents colder for longer. Lunch boxes which are normally stored near hot central heating pipes in school cloakrooms are also a potential problem, in which case you should discuss an alternative storage place with the school.

Below: a healthy packed lunch of juice, fruit, digestive biscuits and wholemeal bread sandwiches

A child who dislikes a 'varied' diet

Some children are simply not interested in what they eat, as long as they don't feel hungry. This can seem worrying with all the advice about encouraging a varied diet. But however nourishing a meal, if left uneaten it is of no nutritional value at all! With such children, it makes more sense to encourage variety in the way a food looks or is served in order to try and stop eating habits from getting into a complete rut. For example, if a child will only eat, say, peanut butter sandwiches in a packed lunch then you could try varying the bread between brown, white and as rolls or crispbreads, to encourage a little more of an adventurous approach to eating.

On the other hand, if lunch is the only meal which is the same each day then there is probably no need to go to these lengths. After all, many people regularly have the same breakfast day after day but enjoy a variety of food at other meals. As long as a child is getting a balanced diet overall, with sufficient variety to meet his nutritional needs, you need not be too concerned.

Food values: SANDWICH FILLINGS		
quantity	protein	fat
ham, 28g (1 oz)	5g	1.5g
salami, 28g (1 oz)	5.5g	13g
liver sausage, 28g (1 oz)	3.5g	7.5g
tongue, 28g (1 oz)	5.5g	6.5g
corned beef, 28g (1 oz)	7.5g	3.5g
Cheddar cheese, 28g (1 oz)	7.5g	10g
Edam, 28g (1 oz)	7.5g	7g
cottage cheese, 28g (1 oz)	4g	1g
peanut butter, 15g (½ oz)	3.5g	8g
tuna, 28g (1 oz)	7g	1.5g

Adventurous packed meals

At midday most children are hungry so the midday meal is important, especially if a child is not a big breakfast eater. A packed lunch should therefore be thought of as the nutritional equivalent of a cold meal so the same rules of meal planning apply — the emphasis being on a variety of 'proper' foods rather than simply a collection of 'fun' foods or snacks.

The biggest problem in providing variety is not so much a lack of ideas as the opinions of school age children who, more often than not, like 'to be the same as everyone else'. Here, it is invaluable if the school and parents can agree a few guidelines such as not allowing sweets, chocolates or soft drinks in school, and having a policy of encouraging children to eat what they are provided with. It is also wise to agree at least five different lunch menus with your child so that her cooperation can be enlisted. She may have some bright ideas of her own, too, and is more likely to eat if she has been involved. What will encourage her most is other children having similar foods to eat (this is an area where school dinners have the advantage over packed lunches).

What to include
Providing a cold meal two or three times a week does not have to be any more complicated than making sandwiches. There are many alternatives to sandwiches which can make the meal more interesting and appealing, and which may in fact take *less* time to prepare. A piece of leftover flan and some cold potatoes from the day before can be the basis of one meal, an extra couple of low-fat sausages can be cooked the day before, a supply of cooked chicken drumsticks can be kept in the freezer and endless salad combinations can be made from small bits of meat, hard-boiled egg, nuts, cold pasta, rice, and vegetables, and so on.

Salads and soups
When providing a salad meal it is important to have a firm container which is the right size so the contents are kept in place, and which has a lid that the child can easily remove without the food flying out. Salads should be of the 'mixed' kind not only because they are more interesting, but also because they will only get jumbled up anyway by the rough treatment usually given to lunch boxes!

Soup may be provided in a thermos flask, but make sure it is either hot or cold — not warm — when you put it in, otherwise bacteria will grow. Flasks also need careful cleaning, especially just below the neck area, where bits of food are easily trapped. A baby bottle brush is useful for getting this area clean.

recipes

GAZPACHO WHIZZ
This can be poured into a vacuum flask or other suitable container, and makes an unusual addition to a summer packed lunch. It can also be used as a fresh-tasting dressing for salads.
Serves 1
140ml (¼ pint) tomato juice
4cm (1½ inch) long chunk of cucumber, washed
1 spring onion, trimmed
1 teaspoon lemon juice
1 teaspoon wine vinegar (optional)
2 teaspoons olive oil
some fresh chopped herbs
pepper
Place all the ingredients, except the pepper, in a blender and whisk together. Season to taste with the pepper. Chill the mixture thoroughly.

EASY NUT NIBBLES
These are good as finger foods, or they can be made into slightly bigger patties as fillings for baps.
Makes 10 bite-sized nibbles
or 6 patties
85g (3 oz) crushed mixed nuts
40g (1½ oz) crushed wheat biscuit cereal
1 teaspoon yeast *or* vegetable extract and 2 teaspoons tomato purée dissolved in 100 ml (3½ fl oz) water
2 medium carrots *or* similar root vegetable, grated
1 tablespoon fresh chopped herbs, such as chives *or* parsley
sesame seeds, toasted (see Method)
In a mixing bowl combine all the ingredients except the sesame seeds. Leave for 5 minutes to allow the liquid to be fully absorbed. Meanwhile, toast the seeds. Heat a non-stick frying pan, add the seeds and cook for 3 to 4 minutes.

Divide the nut mixture into 10 portions and form into balls, squeezing out any surplus liquid. Roll in the sesame seeds. Chill for a few hours to firm.

HUMMUS
Serves 4
1 × 440g (14oz) can chick peas, well drained and rinsed
1 or more cloves garlic, crushed
2 tablespoons lemon juice
1 tablespoon olive *or* corn oil (or similar)
water *or* stock, to blend
Garnish
paprika pepper
chopped parsley *or* mint

Above: Chicken and Pasta Salad, Easy Nut
Nibbles, Gazpacho Whizz, and melon

recipes

Place the chick peas, garlic, lemon juice and oil in a blender or food processor and blend until smooth, adding enough water or stock to make a smooth consistency. (A blender or food processor really is necessary for this recipe, as rubbing the chick peas through a sieve is extremely hard and time-consuming work.)

Pack into suitable containers. Serve with pitta bread and vegetable sticks.

CHICKEN AND PASTA SALAD

You can use whatever quantities you fancy of the ingredients below, according to your preferences and what you have available. Increase the quantity of dressing as necessary, but keep the ingredients in the same proportions.

cold cooked pasta shapes
cold cooked chicken, diced
cooked kidney beans
cooked carrots, chopped
sultanas
raw courgette, chopped
frozen peas, thawed, uncooked
frozen sweetcorn, thawed, uncooked
red pepper, chopped
Dressing
1 tablespoon low-fat mayonnaise
1 tablespoon plain yogurt
2 tablespoons milk
1 teaspoon ground coriander
few drops lemon juice

Make the dressing. Place all the ingredients in a bowl and whisk together. Place all the salad ingredients together in a mixing bowl, pour over some dressing, and turn so that all the ingredients are well coated with dressing.

Pack the salad in suitable containers.

TUNA AND KIDNEY BEAN MIX

Serves 2 to 4

small can tuna, well drained
½ × 400g (14 oz) can kidney beans
drained and rinsed (the other
half can be frozen)
4 small cold potatoes, chopped
¼ cucumber, chopped
1 orange, peeled and chopped
1 apple, washed and chopped
3 tomatoes, chopped
2 or 3 spring onions, trimmed
and chopped
fresh mint, chopped

Place all the ingredients in a bowl, and mix together carefully. The juices from the fruits provide enough moisture and are all the dressing this salad needs.

Pack in suitable containers and accompany with chunks of good bread.

Picnics

Picnics are great fun but they can sometimes be a necessity — as when travelling — and will give all the more pleasure if they are kept simple and easy to manage. Instead of mounds of sandwiches, you could serve wedges of pies and flans, salads scooped into split, halved pitta breads, crunchy vegetable sticks with a dip, croquettes or foods covered in breadcrumbs, such as bite-sized pieces of chicken or turkey, a tasty chilled soup, or plain French bread and cheese.

Foods to avoid

Foods which are probably best avoided on picnics are sticky foods like large pieces of orange, sugar-coated buns, whole tomatoes, anything with a sloppy sauce, and sugary drinks. Also avoid milk drinks if eating in the car as the smell is difficult to get rid of if they get spilt.

Packing a picnic

In order to keep picnic food fresh as well as safe, a cool box is ideal (and will also protect food from being squashed). Cool boxes are kept cool with one or two freezer packs. Items which need to be kept coldest should be put at the bottom of the box with the freezer pack at the top. This is so that the ice pack can maintain a circulation of cool air, since warm air rises and cold air sinks.

Other useful items are a supply of cleansing wipes or a couple of clean wet cloths, and a couple of large plastic bags, one for rubbish and one for dirty utensils and containers to be washed at home.

recipes

PISSALADIÈRE

The pastry in this recipe has one third fat to flour. Self-raising flour helps compensate for the reduced shortening. Wholemeal flour tends to soak up more water so, if you are using it, you may find the traditional proportions of half fat to flour easier to handle.

Makes one 20-23 cm (8-9 inch) flan
Pastry
170g (6 oz) self-raising flour, white, wholemeal *or* a mixture
60g (2 oz) polyunsaturate margarine
1½-2 tablespoons cold water
Filling
2 teaspoons oil
1 clove garlic, peeled and chopped
1 onion, peeled and chopped
1 × 400g (14 oz) tin tomatoes, chopped
2 fresh tomatoes, chopped
3 *or* 4 green tomato 'spiders' (the green stalks), for flavouring
2 *or* 3 sprigs parsley, chopped *or* ½ teaspoon dried mixed herbs
2 eggs, beaten
Garnish
½ × 60g (2 oz) tin anchovy fillets, well-drained
black olives

Place the flour in a bowl and scatter with small knobs of the margarine. Using your fingertips, rub the fat into the flour until it resembles fine breadcrumbs. Add the water and mix the dough into a ball.

Put the pastry in the fridge to allow the water to penetrate more evenly while you prepare the filling.

Place the oil in a large non-stick frying pan, and heat until the oil runs easily. Add the garlic and onion, stir, cover with a lid and allow to soften for a couple of minutes. Add the remaining ingredients, except the egg, bring to the boil, reduce the heat and simmer to allow some tomato juice to evaporate. Remove from the heat and take out the 'spiders'. Leave to cool. Roll out the pastry and line a 20 or 23cm (8 or 9 inch) flan dish.

Add the beaten egg to the tomato mixture, stir thoroughly and pour into the pastry shell. Decorate with the anchovy fillets and olives.

Bake in a preheated fairly hot oven, 190°C (375°F), Gas Mark 5, for 40 minutes, or until the filling feels firm.

SARDINE-STUFFED TOMATOES

Serves 4
8 good-sized tomatoes
Stuffing
1 × 120g (4¼ oz) tin sardines (canned in brine), drained and mashed
4 cm (1½ inch) length cucumber, coarsely chopped
¼ green pepper, finely chopped
2 dessertspoons low-fat mayonnaise
1 dessertspoon low-fat yogurt
1 teaspoon lemon juice
dash tomato ketchup
pinch paprika
1 small clove garlic, crushed (optional)
freshly ground black pepper

In a bowl, combine all the ingredients for the stuffing, mixing well.

Cut the tops off the tomatoes, then hollow out the centres and stuff with the sardine mixture.

COCKTAIL KEBABS

For safety, snip off the ends of the cocktail sticks after threading kebabs.

Thread cocktail sticks with any of the following combinations:
cubes of cheese and pineapple
● cubes of cooked chicken and grapes
● rolled strips of ham and peach chunks ● chopped pieces of frankfurter, cubes of cucumber and triangles of red pepper

AVOCADO DIP

Thinned with a little milk, this delicious dip also makes a good salad dressing.

Serves 4
1 ripe avocado, medium to large size
juice of ½ lemon
freshly ground black pepper
a little plain yogurt

Babies and toddlers

The main problem when travelling with babies is the difficulty of heating up foods. In this case you either need foods which can be served cold, or require only the addition of hot water from a thermos flask to warm them; or you could give your baby a 'breakfast' of wheat biscuit cereal (which absorbs milk and avoids spills), and some fruit.

Right: Avocado Dip, Cocktail Kebabs, Pitta Pockets, Pissaladière

Optional extras
1 clove garlic, crushed
1 small chopped tomato
5cm (2 inch) long chunk of cucumber, chopped
¼ finely chopped red *or* green pepper
Scoop out the avocado flesh into a mixing bowl, and mash with the lemon juice and pepper. Add any extra ingredients and thin with a little yogurt. Pack into a suitable container, and serve with raw vegetables or bread sticks.

PITTA POCKETS

Halved and split pitta breads can be filled with various mixes to create slightly more unusual, but easy-to-make, 'sandwiches' for a picnic. Place the fillings in separate containers, and spoon into the pitta bread just before eating, so the bread does not become soggy.

Here are some fillings you could try:
shredded lettuce, Mozzarella slices, orange segments and chopped walnuts ● chickpeas and coleslaw ● shredded lettuce, chopped, hard-boiled egg, chopped tuna, onion rings, chopped tomato and chives ● Tuna and Kidney Bean Mix (see page 45) ● Many Bean Salad (see page 62) ● shredded lettuce and cottage cheese mixed with yeast extract *or* vegetable extract

Family meals

Family meals are a valuable part of family life. One of their most important advantages is a social one because they provide an opportunity for everyone to be together. Children can be allowed to participate by laying the table, washing vegetables and passing dishes. Food in serving dishes, which children can serve themselves, not only allows them to enjoy a feeling of independence, but also helps them to become familiar with new 'grown-up' foods. It must also be said that family meals can be the bane of many parents' lives if they have to cope with the family's varying likes and dislikes; but if a bowl of salad or fruit and a basket of bread are also served with meals there will always be something for fussy eaters to choose from.

recipes

Grains and nuts

One of the commonest traditional foods made from grains is wheat flour, most often eaten as bread or pastry as well as in a sweetened form in cakes and biscuits. Bread is a particularly healthy food which we should all eat more of, whereas pastry tends to be a fatty food and so is better eaten less frequently.

Bread and flour

If you eat bread at most meals, there is no need for it always to be wholemeal as this can get boring which, in turn, will mean that less bread is likely to get eaten. There is a great variety of tasty breads available which you can try out. These may be made from different flours such as rye or oats; made with added herbs, onions, milk, or wholegrains; or topped with cracked wheat or seeds like poppy and sesame.

Rice and pasta

There are many varieties of rice and pasta in the shops, too. Brown rice takes about 10 minutes longer than white rice to cook, but it has much more flavour and texture and the grains do not stick together so easily.

Other grains

There are other grain foods besides bread, flour, rice and pasta which, if used as a change, could add variety and interest to many dishes. Barley makes a good addition to soups and stews and has a pleasant flavour when cooked as flakes for a milk pudding. Bulgar or cracked wheat is already partially cooked. It takes only 15 to 20 minutes to cook and makes a tasty alternative to rice in salads. Millet takes 30 to 40 minutes to cook and can be used in the same way. Like rice, millet is gluten-free and so is particularly valuable for those who are allergic to wheat.

Oats have a distinctive flavour and are sold as oatmeal grains or as porridge oat 'flakes'. Oats have many other uses besides being made into the traditional porridge. Porridge oats can be

recipes

PILAFF VEGETABLE RICE

Serves 4

110g (4 oz) each of carrots and onions peeled and chopped
110g (4 oz) each of courgettes and French beans, washed, trimmed and chopped
1 clove garlic, peeled and crushed
110g (4 oz) brown rice
60g (2 oz) unsalted peanuts (omit for under-fives)
pinch mixed herbs
1 bay leaf
1 dessertspoon oil
salt and freshly ground black pepper

Place all the vegetables (except the courgettes) and the garlic in a saucepan and just cover with boiling water. Add the rice, nuts (add separately later if feeding an under-five), herbs and oil. Bring to the boil, reduce the heat, and allow to simmer for about 30 minutes.

Remove the saucepan lid 5 minutes before the end of the cooking time, add the courgettes, and bring to the boil to evaporate any excess water. Season to taste with salt and pepper. Serve in a warmed dish.

VEGETABLE CRUMBLE

Serves 4

1 tablespoon oil
1 large onion, peeled and chopped
2 cloves garlic, peeled and chopped
2 carrots, scraped and diced
1 leek, washed and cut in rings
1 stick celery, scrubbed and thinly sliced
100g (3½ oz) broccoli, broken into florets
100g (3½ oz) button mushrooms, wiped and halved
½ × 400g (14 oz) tin kidney beans, drained and rinsed,
or 4 rashers bacon, cooked and chopped
½ teaspoon dried herbs
420ml (¾ pint) water, mixed with
1 tablespoon tomato purée
salt and pepper
Crumble topping
120g (4 oz) wholemeal flour
60g (2 oz) soft margarine
4 tablespoons rolled oats
1 tablespoon sesame seeds

Place the oil in a saucepan, add the onion and garlic, and sauté. Add the remaining vegetables, except the beans. Stir, cover and allow to sweat. When the broccoli has turned a brighter green and the mushrooms are soft, add the herbs and the tomato-flavoured water.

Replace the lid, bring to the boil, reduce the heat and simmer for about 20 minutes, or until the vegetables are soft. Add the beans or bacon, and season.

While the vegetables are cooking, make the crumble topping. Place the flour in a bowl and rub in the margarine with your fingertips until the mixture resembles coarse breadcrumbs (or do this in a food processor). Add the oats and sesame seeds.

Pour into a deep greased ovenproof dish, sprinkle over the crumble topping and bake in a preheated moderate oven, 180°C (350°F), Gas Mark 4, for 25 to 30 minutes.

PEANUT BUTTER SAUCE

Nut sauces, like this and the one that follows, are surprisingly strong-flavoured so a little goes a long way. Served hot, they are good with rice, pasta, potato cakes, baked fish and steamed vegeta-

added to savoury or sweet crumbles to help lighten them. Oatmeal can be added to pastry to vary the texture. It also makes a good coating for croquettes and rissoles.

Right: Vegetable Crumble

Nuts and seeds

Nuts and seeds are rich in fats, unlike grains, with the exception of chestnuts which are very low in fat. Hazelnuts have two-thirds the fat of other nuts. The fat is usually of the healthier unsaturated type, with the exception of coconut fat which is highly saturated. Nuts and seeds are also rich in protein, fibre, vitamins and minerals and are quick to cook.

bles. When cold, nut sauces make tasty dips for raw vegetables.

Makes 140ml (5fl oz)

4 teaspoons peanut butter
110ml (4fl oz) water, flavoured
with a little tomato purée
2 teaspoons lemon juice

For a cold dressing, process, or whisk, the ingredients together.

To serve as a hot sauce, place the peanut butter in a saucepan and heat gently. Stir in the water and lemon juice.

CASHEW AND GINGER SAUCE

Makes 140-300 ml (¼-½ pint)

60g (2 oz) cashew nuts, toasted
(see Method)
¼-½ teaspoon freshly
grated ginger
1 teaspoon soy sauce
140-275ml (¼ to ½ pint) milk *or* water

To toast the nuts, toss in a greased non-stick frying pan over a gentle heat.

Place the ingredients and 140ml (¼ pint) of milk or water in a blender, and blend until smooth. Pour into a saucepan and heat, stirring. Add more water or milk to achieve the right consistency.

Pulses and roots

Pulses — that is, peas and beans — are rich in protein, fibre, minerals and some vitamins. Most are low in fat, the exception being soya beans. Some pulses are eaten fresh — notably peas, beans of various kinds and beansprouts. Fresh beans are lower in protein than dried beans but richer in vitamins.

Preparing beans
Most beans need to be soaked for about 8 hours, but not too long or they will start to ferment. This process can sometimes be speeded up by soaking in hot, boiled water for a couple of hours. *All beans should be fast-boiled for 10 minutes in fresh water*, and then simmered for the required length of time. Mung beans and lentils do not need soaking. Proper preparation of beans is vital in order to deactivate the natural toxins which some contain.

Beans and 'wind'
Beans contain an uncommon form of sugar which tends to produce quantities of gas in the intestines. Provided beans are properly prepared, most people find their digestive systems learn to cope with them better once they are established in the diet.

Growing beansprouts
Growing beansprouts, like growing cress, is an activity children much enjoy. All you have to do is to put some beans like mung, aduki or whole lentils in a jam jar, cover them with water and leave them in a warm place. The beans need to be drained and rinsed with fresh water twice a day. Beansprouts are good scattered on hot, thick soups as well as in salads.

Coping with a vegetarian
It is not uncommon for children in meat-eating families to go through a vegetarian stage. Being 'vegetarian' to them may simply mean not eating those cuts of meat that clearly look like what they are. A convenient way of coping with this is to prepare vegetarian meals for the whole family, but divide the dishes into two portions, with one part having some highly flavoured meat or fish added as an extra.

Below: Bean Paella with Prawns

recipes

BEAN PAELLA WITH PRAWNS

Serves 4 to 6

60g (2 oz) dried mung beans
225g (8 oz) brown rice
550 ml (1 pint) water
1 small aubergine, washed and diced
2 tablespoons oil
1 onion, peeled and chopped
2 cloves garlic, peeled and chopped
2 carrots, scraped and diced
1 stick celery, scrubbed and
thinly sliced
1 green pepper, washed,
deseeded and chopped
110g (4 oz) button mushrooms, wiped
and quartered
1 × 400g (14 oz) tin tomatoes, drained
200g (7 oz) cooked *or* tinned and
drained kidney beans
Garnish
60g (2 oz) prawns

Rinse the mung beans, and soak in cold water for 2 hours. (You can omit the soaking but the beans may be a bit 'windy'.) Drain. Place in a saucepan with fresh water to cover. Bring to the boil and cook for 10 minutes, then reduce the heat and simmer for 10 to 20 minutes.

Pour the water into a saucepan, bring to the boil, add the rice and cook for 30 minutes. If the raw aubergine tastes bitter, sprinkle it with a little salt and let it 'weep' to remove the bitter juices.

Heat the oil in a large pan or casserole. Add the onion and garlic and sauté for a few minutes. Add the carrots, celery, green pepper and aubergine (patted dry if it has been salted). Cover and cook for 10 minutes. Add the mushrooms and the tomatoes, and cook for 5 minutes.

Combine the cooked rice, mung beans and kidney beans with the vegetables. Season with salt and pepper if you wish. Cook gently for a further 15 minutes.

Turn into a serving dish, garnish, and serve with a green salad.

Variation You can substitute 110g (4 oz) cooked chick peas or whole lentils for the mung beans.

GRANNY'S VEGETABLE SOUP

Serves 6

1 dessertspoon oil
225g (8 oz) carrots, scraped and
chopped
225g (8 oz) potatoes, peeled
and chopped
225g (8 oz) frozen peas
1 large onion, peeled and chopped
1 litre (1¾ pints) good stock, *or* water
mixed with 1 chicken stock cube
freshly ground black pepper

Place the oil in a pressure cooker or large saucepan, add the vegetables and allow to sweat for a few minutes. Add the stock, place the lid on the pressure cooker and cook for 5 minutes. If using an ordinary saucepan, bring to the boil, reduce the heat and simmer for 30 minutes, or until the vegetables are soft.

Season and blend to a smooth consistency, or rub through a sieve.

CHICK PEAS WITH RICE

Serves 2 to 4

100g (3½ oz) brown rice
275ml (½ pint) water
1 tablespoon oil (olive preferably)
1 large onion
2 cloves garlic
1 × 400g (14 oz) tin chick peas,
drained and rinsed, *or* 280g (10 oz)
cooked chick peas
freshly ground black pepper

Pour the water into a saucepan, bring to the boil, add the rice and cook for about 30 minutes, or until the water is absorbed. Drain the rice.

Meanwhile heat the oil in a non-stick frying pan, add the onion and garlic, and sauté gently, but do not allow to burn. Add the chick peas, cover, and allow to heat through for about 5 minutes.

Turn into a serving bowl, mix with the rice and season with pepper. Serve with a crisp salad, dressed with Oil and Fruit Juice Dressing (see page 62).

Variation Pasta may be used instead of rice, if preferred.

SPLIT PEA SHEPHERD'S PIE

Serves 4

225g (8 oz) yellow *or* green split peas,
washed and soaked for 6-8 hours
550ml (1 pint) stock
1 tablespoon oil
1 medium onion, peeled and chopped
1 clove garlic, chopped
2 carrots, scraped and thinly sliced
2 sticks celery, scrubbed and
thinly sliced
1 red pepper, deseeded and chopped
100g (3½ oz) mushrooms, wiped
and chopped
3 tablespoons chopped tinned tomato
1 teaspoon dried mixed herbs
¼ teaspoon nutmeg
salt and freshly ground black pepper
Topping
1kg (2¼lb) potatoes, peeled or
scrubbed
4-5 tablespoons milk
30g (1oz) grated cheese
salt and freshly ground black pepper
2 large tomatoes

Drain the split peas, place in a saucepan with the stock and cook for about 1 hour.

Meanwhile place the potatoes for the topping in a saucepan of boiling water, and boil until cooked.

Heat the oil in a saucepan and add the onion, garlic, carrots, celery and pepper. Cover and cook for about 15 minutes, or until the vegetables soften. Add the mushrooms and cook for another minute. Mix in the cooked split peas, tinned tomato, herbs and nutmeg. Season. Turn the mixture into a large greased pie dish.

Mash the cooked potatoes adding the milk, cheese and seasoning. Beat well and spread over the pea mixture.

Cut the tomatoes in half, crosswise, and arrange them on the potato, cut side uppermost, pushing them down into the topping. Bake in a preheated fairly hot oven, 190°C (375°F), Gas Mark 5, for 20 to 25 minutes, or until the topping is brown. Serve with green cabbage.

Fish

Fish is a highly nutritious food. The white kinds are particularly lean and digestible and the oily kinds – herring, sardines, trout, mackerel and salmon – have constituents which, if eaten two or three times a week, are particularly beneficial for the heart. Oily fish is also amongst the very few foods naturally rich in vitamin D. The soft bones are a good source of calcium too. Smoked fish have the disadvantage that they are very salty and this saltiness may need 'diluting' by combining the fish with other foods, as in fish pie where smoked fish can provide a useful extra flavour.

Buying and storing fish

When buying fresh fish, the best way to judge the quality is by looking at the shop which sells it. If the assistants have clean clothes and nails and the fish is kept on plenty of ice, with clear separation of ready-to-eat products like smoked salmon from raw fish, then the fish should be well looked after. Fresh fish should look shiny, firm, have bright red gills and have no trace of ammonia (like wet nappies) in its smell. The fishmonger will be able to fillet any fish for you as well as advising you on how to cook unfamiliar types.

At home, fresh fish should be unwrapped, put in a covered bowl (to allow air to circulate and to prevent fishy smells from penetrating other foods) and stored at the bottom of the fridge until it is needed.

Cooking fish

Fish cooks best if done quickly at a gentle heat. Fresh fish cooked in a closed container or roasting bag presents little problem with smells. It should always be eaten on the day of purchase because it stales quickly. The 'off' smells and tastes you may notice are produced by bacteria, but do not usually make the fish (except shellfish) unsafe to eat. For this reason fish can be marinated and safely eaten raw.

Coping with bones

The biggest drawback of fresh fish, particularly with children, are the bones. The easiest fish to debone are probably monkfish, huss and fish steaks like cod, hake and salmon. In these products, the bones are usually large and easily identifiable. Round fish like trout can be fairly easily boned if a knife is slid along the spine of the cooked fish and the meat is lifted away from the spine and down the ribs. Starting from the belly side of the fish can cause the more fragile ends of the rib bones to snap off.

Food values: FISH		
quantity: 100g (3½ oz)	protein	fat
cod/haddock, grilled, baked, poached	21g	1.5g
kipper/smoked mackerel	25.5g	11.5g
trout	23g	4.5g
cod/haddock, battered	20g	10.5g
prawns	22.5g	2g
sardines, tinned in oil and drained	23.5g	13.5g
plaice, steamed	19g	2g
plaice, fried in crumbs	13.5g	8.5g
fish fingers, grilled	12.5g	7.5g
fish fingers, fried	13.5g	12.5g

recipes

FISH CAKES

Leftover fish pie can be used as the base for this, though if this includes sauce then extra potato may be needed to mop it up and make a firmer mixture.

Makes 4

280g (10oz) potatoes cooked and mashed
100g (3½oz) cooked fish (such as cod, smoked haddock, trout, fish pie) *or*
1 × 100g (3½oz) tin salmon, drained
2 tablespoons cooked vegetables (such as peas, carrots, sweetcorn, cabbage), chopped if necessary
porridge oats (optional, see Method)
1 egg (optional, see Method)
flour, for coating
1 dessertspoon oil, for frying

Place the potatoes, fish and vegetables in a mixing bowl, and mix until well blended. If the mixture is too moist add some porridge oats; if it crumbles too easily, add a small beaten egg. Divide into four, shape into cakes and dust with flour to prevent sticking.

Heat the oil in a non-stick frying pan. When the oil runs easily, brush it over the surface of the pan. Any excess oil should be poured off. Add the fish cakes to the pan and cook until nicely browned on both sides, about 15 minutes.

Serve with a green vegetable and halved tomatoes, either grilled or cooked in the pan with the fish cakes.

MONKFISH WITH GARLIC

Monkfish is a firm-fleshed fish which is easy to bone, and is ideal for someone who prefers meat or who is frightened of bones. Huss is a less expensive alternative to monkfish.

Serves 4

4 pieces of monkfish tail *or* steaks
juice of ½ lemon
2 cloves garlic, crushed
freshly ground black pepper

Remove any skin from the fish, if not already done by fishmonger. Wash and pat the fish dry. Sprinkle with the lemon juice, garlic and pepper. Then either microwave, grill or bake.

To microwave, place the monkfish in a dish, cover with clingfilm or a damp piece of kitchen towel, and cook on Full

Above: *Fish Cake with tomato, peas and sweetcorn*

recipes

for 4 to 5 minutes. To grill, cook on both sides for 8 to 10 minutes altogether, turning once, until the flesh near the bone is soft and white and comes away when prodded with a knife (overcooking makes it rubbery). To bake, cover and cook in a preheated hot oven, 230°C (450°F), Gas Mark 8, for 15 to 20 minutes.

Serve garnished with parsley and lemon wedges.

COD STEAKS WITH FENNEL SAUCE

Frozen cod steaks are a useful standby and, unless you are very unlucky, they are usually bone-free. The aniseed-like flavour of the sauce complements the blandness of the fish.

Serves 4
4 frozen cod steaks
juice of ½ lemon
salt and pepper
Sauce
2 fennel bulbs, washed and chopped
2 small potatoes, peeled and chopped
1 onion, peeled and chopped
275ml (½ pint) chicken stock
freshly ground pepper

First make the sauce. Place the vegetables and stock in a pan, cover, bring to the boil, reduce the heat and simmer for 30 minutes. Pureé in a processor, or press through a sieve. (If you use a liquidizer, pureé a little at a time, or pockets of steam may cause the sauce to 'explode' out of the top of the container, with the risk of burning.

Meanwhile, place the cod steaks in a greased dish, and sprinkle with the lemon juice and seasoning. Cover and bake in a preheated moderate oven 180°C (350°F), Gas Mark 4, for about 20 minutes. Check that it is cooked by inserting a knife into the flesh: if the fish is properly cooked, it will be creamy white all through.

Arrange the steaks on a serving dish, pour over the sauce and serve.

KEDGEREE

Serves 2 generously, or 4 if portions are smaller
140g (5oz) brown rice
420ml (¾ pint) water
salt and pepper
1×200g (7oz) boil-in-the-bag smoked haddock
1 dessertspoon oil
1 onion, peeled and chopped
½ teaspoon curry powder *or* garam masala
1-2 hard-boiled eggs, finely chopped

Place the water in a saucepan and bring to the boil. Add the rice, stir, reduce the heat, cover and simmer for 30 minutes, by which time all the water should have been absorbed. If necessary, add extra water 5 minutes before the end of the cooking time, or increase the heat if there is still too much water.

Meanwhile, boil the bag of fish according to the instructions on the packet. Heat the oil in a non-stick frying pan, add the onion and sauté until it begins to go golden brown. Stir in the curry powder or garam masala and cook for a further minute. Remove from the heat, add the cooked fish and keep warm.

Tip the rice into a warmed dish and make a well in the centre. Pour in the fish and onions, garnish with egg and serve with a green salad.

55

Poultry

Chicken is a naturally lean meat and turkey is even leaner. In both, the fat is mainly found in the skin and within the body cavity, where it can be easily removed. Wild game birds like pheasant are also lean, whereas domesticated duck and goose are very fatty. Poultry, like fish, is a highly nutritious food. Turkey is also becoming as versatile as beef and is increasingly being sold as fillets, escalopes and cutlets, or diced or minced. Because turkey meat is less tough than the cheaper cuts of beef it requires much less cooking time.

The risk of food poisoning
Although poultry is commonly infected with *Salmonella* it presents no problem provided the bird is cooked properly and, in the case of frozen birds, defrosted thoroughly beforehand. The body cavity is the riskiest part of the bird because this area is easily contaminated and, during cooking, takes a long while to get thoroughly hot, enabling bacteria to flourish in the meantime. For this reason it is unwise to stuff poultry: in order to cook the stuffing properly, you will need to cook the bird for longer, and then the outside is likely to have dried out and lost its flavour.

Bacterial contamination is not a problem in the middle of a solid lump of meat (unless it has been pierced by a contaminated skewer or knife), which is why joints of beef can safely be cooked 'rare', if wished.

Whole *unstuffed* birds can be cooked quickly if casseroled. This is because the cooking juices penetrate the cavity and so cooking takes place from the inside as well as the outside.

Food values: POULTRY		
quantity: 100g (3½ oz)	protein	fat
turkey, light meat	30g	1.5g
turkey, dark meat	28g	4g
chicken	25g	5.5g
roast chicken with skin	22.5g	14g
duck, meat only	25g	9.5g
duck, meat, fat and skin	20g	29g

Below: Stir-fry Celery Chicken

recipes

TURKEY FILLETS IN HERBY BREADCRUMBS

Serves 4

450g (1lb) turkey fillet about 1cm (½ inch) or more thick, cut into 2.5cm (1 inch) strips

Coating

3 heaped tablespoons wholemeal flour, seasoned with pepper

1 egg beaten with a little milk, and with a generous squeeze of garlic pureé (optional)

100g (3½ oz) wholemeal breadcrumbs mixed with a handful of chopped parsley and a tablespoon ground coriander

Dip each turkey strip into the flour, then into the egg, then roll in the bread-crumbs. Place on a greased baking tray and bake in a preheated hot oven, 220°C (425°F), Gas Mark 7, for 10 minutes.

STIR-FRY CELERY CHICKEN

Serves 2 to 3

2 tablespoons oil, plus a little extra (see Method)

2 spring onions, trimmed and chopped

225g (8oz) raw chicken, boned and shredded

170g (6oz) celery, scrubbed and very finely cut diagonally

100g (3½oz) carrots, washed and cut into small thin strips

⅓ cup water

Seasoning

a little salt

⅓ teaspoon sugar

1 teaspoon light soy sauce

1 teaspoon oil

pinch of pepper

Combine the seasoning ingredients in a large bowl. Add the chicken, turn in the seasoning to coat, and leave to marinate for 20 minutes.

Heat the oil in a non-stick frying pan, add the spring onions, and quickly stir-fry. Then add the chicken, and stir-fry until cooked through. Remove the chicken and onions from the pan and set aside. There should still be almost the same amount of oil left in the pan, but add extra if necessary and reheat.

Stir-fry the celery, then add the carrots to the pan and sprinkle with the water. Stir well, cover and cook for 2 minutes, or until the vegetables are soft.

Return the chicken and onions to the pan and stir-fry again until hot. Mix well and serve with rice or noodles.

CHICKEN AND VEGETABLE LOAF

Serves 3 to 4

340g (12oz) cooked chicken, chopped into 1cm (½ inch) chunks

1 carrot, either cooked and chopped or scrubbed and thinly sliced

6 French beans, washed and trimmed

Sauce

1 teaspoon oil

170g (6oz) mushrooms, wiped and chopped

1 small onion, peeled and well chopped

170ml (6fl oz) good stock, *or* water mixed with 1 teaspoon vegetable *or* chicken extract

1 rounded tablespoon wholemeal flour

salt and pepper

First make the sauce. Heat the oil in a non-stick frying pan, add the mushrooms and onion and allow to sweat. Add 140ml (5fl oz) stock, bring to the boil, reduce the heat and simmer for 3 minutes.

Mix the flour with the remaining stock and add to the pan. Stir and cook until the sauce has thickened. Season with salt and pepper, and stir in the chicken.

Grease a 1kg (2lb) loaf tin (it may help to line the base and ends with a strip of well-greased foil) and add half the sauce. Press down. Lay the carrot and beans lengthwise on top. Finally add the remaining chicken mixture and press down. Bake the loaf in a preheated fairly hot oven 190°C (375°F), Gas Mark 5, for 30 minutes.

Leave to cool in the tin and chill. Run a knife along the unlined edges and invert the loaf on to a serving plate. Cut into slices with a sharp knife.

LEMON CHICKEN CASSEROLE

Serves 4

1 carrot, scraped and sliced

1 celery stick, scrubbed and thinly sliced

1 onion, peeled and thinly sliced

1 bayleaf

juice of ½ lemon, plus extra if necessary (see Method)

550ml (1 pint) water

1 small chicken, skinned, wiped and cut into 8 joints (you could ask your butcher to do this, or buy chicken joints)

Sauce

275ml (½ pint) reserved cooking liquid (see Method)

1 rounded tablespoon white flour

salt and pepper

4 tablespoons plain yogurt, to garnish

Place the carrot, celery, onion, bayleaf, lemon juice and water in a large sauce-pan and bring to the boil. Add the chicken, cover and simmer for 45 minutes to 1 hour. To check that the chicken is cooked, pierce the thickest parts with a skewer: no pink juices should come out. Remove the chicken and keep warm.

Taste the stock and add a little more lemon juice if liked. Boil the stock to reduce it by half, to 275ml (½ pint), to strengthen the flavour. Strain, and discard the vegetables.

Pour the reduced stock into a sauce-pan. Blend the flour to a smooth paste with a little water. Stir in some of the warm stock and add to the pan. Bring to the boil, stirring occasionally, then simmer for 10 minutes, or until the sauce thickens. Season with salt and pepper.

Arrange the chicken pieces on a serving dish, pour over the sauce, and then the yogurt.

Meat

Lean meat is rich in protein but is perhaps more valued for the minerals it contains, like iron and zinc. In meat these minerals are in a form which is easiest for the human body to absorb. Cheaper cuts and meat products can be very fatty, which means they contain fewer nutrients because there is less actual 'meat'.

Buying meat

Unfortunately the word 'meat' on a label can mean both organ and muscle tissue and fat. Some supermarkets now label the fat content of the mince they sell. On average mince contains 16 per cent fat, whereas ground steak is usually closer to 10 per cent. Some meats, even lean ones, are much fattier than others. For example, lean beef is on average 4–12 per cent fat, liver 6–10 per cent, lean pork 7–10 per cent while lean lamb has the highest average fat content of 8–16 per cent (people appear to be eating less lamb nowadays).

When buying cooked meats from a butcher it is very important to check that they have been kept well away from raw meats as this can lead to bacterial contamination.

Cooking meat

The tenderness of meat is increased the more it is pounded, beaten and ground: it is this sort of physical punishment which breaks up the fibres. Marinating can only soften the outside of meat, and does not affect the tissues inside. Long, slow cooking or cooking in a microwave also tenderizes the cheaper cuts of meat by turning the collagen or gristle which is present into a soft gel. Long slow cooking of good-quality cuts of meat, on the other hand, merely drys out and toughens them.

Food values: **MEAT**		
quantity: 100g (3½ oz)	protein	fat
roast beef, lean	27.5g	9g
grilled steak, lean	28.5g	6g
mince	20-26g	10-20g
roast lamb	20g	26g
roast pork, lean	31g	7g
roast pork with crackling	27g	20g
gammon, lean	30g	5.5g
venison	35g	6.5g

recipes

BEEF AND VEGETABLE STEW WITH MUSTARD BREAD

This dish creates its own delicious sauce and the best part is the mustard-coated bread which mops up the juice.

Serves 3 to 4

1 dessertspoon oil
1 onion, peeled and chopped
350g (12oz) lean diced braising steak
1 leek, washed, trimmed and sliced
3 medium carrots, scraped and sliced
1 large parsnip *or* 2 small ones, peeled and chopped
2 celery sticks, washed and thinly sliced
1 tablespoon tomato purée
2 bay leaves
½ teaspoon mixed herbs
420 to 550ml (¾ to 1 pint) boiling water
3 to 4 thick slices bread
some mild mustard mixed with a little horseradish, if liked

Place the oil in a large saucepan and heat until it runs. Add the onion and sauté until soft and golden. Add the meat and cook until brown, stirring frequently. Add the leek, carrots, parsnip and celery and allow to sweat for 3 to 4 minutes.

Transfer the meat and vegetables to an ovenproof dish, add the tomato purée and herbs and pour in sufficient boiling water to almost cover the ingredients. Place on the middle to lower shelf of a preheated cool oven, 150°C (300°F), Gas Mark 2, and leave to simmer for 2 hours.

Just before serving, toast the bread and spread lightly with the mustard. Place a slice of toast on each plate, and ladle out the stew on top. Serve with baked potatoes and a green vegetable.

Variation For a special occasion you can use venison instead of beef.

PORK AND BEANS

The gammon stock in this recipe makes the beans taste succulent and less floury. It is worth doing some extra beans at the same time and freezing those you don't immediately need.

Serves 6

450g (1lb) dried haricot beans
stock *or* water, as required (see Method)
1 carrot, scraped and chopped in half
1 onion, peeled and stuck with 4 cloves
1 clove garlic, peeled
1 bouquet garni
450g (1lb) gammon *or* boiling bacon
4 frankfurters, chopped
tomato purée (optional, see Method)

Soak the beans in water for about 6 to 8 hours. Drain. Place in a saucepan with some fresh water to cover, bring to the boil and boil for 10 minutes.

Drain and return to the pan with the stock or water, carrot, onion, garlic, bouquet garni and gammon or bacon. There should be enough liquid to just cover all the ingredients. Bring to the boil, cover, reduce the heat and gently simmer for about 1 hour.

Remove the gammon (or bacon) and reserve. Discard the carrot, onion, garlic and bouquet garni. Chop the gammon (or bacon) into small pieces and return to the pan with the frankfurters. Cook gently for

recipes

at least another 30 minutes. Make sure you keep the casserole moist, if necessary adding extra water mixed with a little tomato purée.

MINCE ROLL

This is a good dish for children who are not over-keen on savoury meat dishes. It is also extremely quick and easy to make, and provides a cheaper alternative to a 'whole' piece of meat.

Serves 3

225g (8oz) lean minced beef
100g (3½oz) carrot, finely diced *or* grated
100g (3½oz) parsnip, finely diced *or* grated
1 medium onion, peeled and chopped

Below: Beef and Vegetable Stew with Mustard Bread, served with beans and potatoes

1 heaped tablespoon oatmeal *or* rolled oats
5 tablespoons water
½ to 1 teaspoon beef *or* vegetable extract
½ tablespoon tomato purée
½ tablespoon brown sauce *or* finely chopped chutney
freshly ground black pepper

Place all the ingredients in a bowl and mix together thoroughly. Pile the mixture on a length of foil and shape into a roll. Wrap the foil around the roll, making sure the edges are tightly secured. Bake in a preheated moderate oven, 180°C (350°F), Gas Mark 4, for 1¼ hours.

Serve with mashed potatoes and a green vegetable or salad.

MEATBALLS WITH TOMATO SAUCE

Makes 12

170g (6oz) lean beef mince
170g (6oz) turkey mince
60 g (2oz) wholemeal breadcrumbs
1 onion, peeled and finely chopped
1 clove garlic, crushed
grated rind of ½ lemon
freshly ground black pepper
Tomato Sauce (see page 73)

Mix all the ingredients together in a large bowl. Shape the mixture into balls, about the size of a 'ping-pong' ball.

Pour the sauce into the bottom of a greased baking dish and arrange the meatballs on top. Cook in a preheated moderately hot oven, at 190°C (375°F), Gas Mark 5, for 30 minutes.

Side vegetables

Vegetables and fruit are particularly important for the vitamins they provide. Unlike other foods, they provide Vitamin C and some are rich sources of Vitamin A and folic acid (a B vitamin) as well. They are also valuable as an important source of fibre.

Vegetables and fruit may well have significant health benefits. Many experts believe there is good evidence that more raw or lightly cooked fruits and vegetables in the diet would help protect against some of the harmful effects of fat, which in turn would give some protection against heart disease and several common cancers.

If you don't have much in the way of vegetables or fruit in your diet, do whatever you can to increase your consumption of these foods. Encouraging the family to eat more fruit may be easier than getting them to eat more vegetables, but you can do a lot to make vegetables more appealing by the way you cook and present them.

Storage
Vegetables are living organisms which, if treated roughly, will perish all the quicker. Most need cool surroundings, some protection from drying out without being actually moist, and gentle handling. Food

technology has developed remarkable ways of keeping vegetables 'fresher' for longer. Packaging foods, in a sealed container with a special mixture of gases, all of which occur naturally in the air, and then chilling them can prolong their shelf life considerably. Of course, buying vegetables packaged in this way from larger food shops and supermarkets can cost more than buying them loose from your local greengrocer.

During storage, foods continue to ripen or age, changing in certain ways as they do so. In vegetables, the sugars found in the young, tender varieties turn to less tasty and sometimes

recipes

SWEDE IN ORANGE JUICE
Serves 4
450g (1lb) swede, peeled and diced
110ml (4 fl oz) orange juice
chopped parsley *or* chives, to garnish
Place the swede and juice in a saucepan and add enough boiling water to just cover the vegetables. Bring to the boil, reduce the heat and simmer gently, uncovered, until cooked and the liquid is reduced to a glaze.

Serve the swede garnished with chopped parsley and chives.

BRAISED CARROT AND POTATO
Serves 4
1 teaspoon oil
1 large onion, peeled and sliced in thin rings
450g (1lb) carrots, scraped and cut into rings
450g (1lb) potatoes, peeled *or* scrubbed and cut into chunks (waxy *or* new potatoes if possible)
50ml (3½ tablespoons) boiling water
chopped fresh coriander, to garnish
Place the oil in a non-stick saucepan, and heat until it runs easily. Add the onion,

stir, cover, reduce the heat and allow the onion to soften for a few minutes.

Add the remaining vegetables and the water. Cover and cook over a medium heat for about 40 minutes, or until the vegetables are tender and the water is absorbed. Avoid stirring the vegetables towards the end of the cooking time or you risk breaking up the potato.

Turn into a serving dish and garnish with the coriander.

STIR-FRY SPINACH WITH GARLIC
This is a recipe for those who do not normally like spinach.
Serves 6
1 tablespoon oil
750g (1½lb) spinach, stalks removed, well washed and drained
2 cloves garlic, peeled and crushed
1 teaspoon sugar
Heat the oil in a large saucepan. Add as much spinach as you can and stir-fry, adding more as it wilts, so that as much of it as possible gets coated with the oil. This will take 2 to 4 minutes depending on the size of the saucepan.

Allow the spinach to cook and wilt

down to about one third of its original volume. Chop roughly, stir in the garlic and sugar and cook for no more than 5 minutes. Drain and serve.

RED CABBAGE WITH FRUIT
This is good hot or cold, and freezes well.
Serves 4
450g (1lb) red cabbage, washed and shredded
1 onion, peeled and chopped
1 tablespoon oil
50ml (3½ tablespoons) wine vinegar
1 large apple, washed, cored and chopped
1 pear *or* apple washed, cored and chopped, *or* juice and zest from 2 small oranges
30g (1oz) sugar
freshly ground black pepper
Place the oil in a large pan with a well-fitting lid, and heat until it runs easily. Add the onion, cover and allow to soften.

Add the remaining ingredients. Bring to the boil, reduce the heat, cover and simmer gently for about 1 hour, or until the liquid is absorbed, stirring every now and again.

*Above: Red Cabbage with
Fruit and Braised Carrot
and Potato*

stringy starches, whereas the opposite is true of fruits. Here, the hard starches of the young fruits get converted into soft sugars as they ripen.

Preparation and cooking
Vegetables should be carefully prepared, as incorrect preparation can affect their nutritional value. They should be washed thoroughly under cold running water, scrubbed, scraped or peeled as necessary, and any discoloured areas and blemishes removed. Vegetables should be cut up as late as possible, or many of the vitamins will be lost from the cut edges. Soaking them in water should be avoided; they should also be cooked in as little boiling water as possible. Cooking in small amounts of water in a pan with a close-fitting lid is similar to steaming and so helps to preserve the nutrients.

Instead of salt, there are numerous flavourings you can use to enhance the taste of vegetables. Try herbs like mint with potatoes and cauliflower; parsley with carrots and turnips; nutmeg or caraway with cabbage, spinach and broccoli; and chives, coriander, paprika and black pepper on almost anything. Whatever you choose, fresh herbs are nicest. You can try experimenting with all sorts of combinations, but if the vegetables are of good quality and have been only lightly cooked, they should taste wonderful on their own without any extras of any sort.

Salads

It is a good rule to have some raw vegetables or fruit every day, and a salad of vegetables mixed with fruit can be a particularly colourful, crunchy and tasty way to achieve this. Most children like raw vegetables and, if their palates have not been dulled by highly sweetened foods and drinks, they will love their natural sweetness.

When choosing vegetables and fruit, avoid any that are dull, wilted, wet, limp or discoloured. Fresh, good-quality fruits and vegetables should look bright, plump and tempting.

Preparation

Because salads are always best when freshest it is better to make them yourself rather than buy 'ready-mades'. Making your own is also safer since there will be less chance of contamination, and you will have a greater choice of ingredients.

Dressing a salad

As with properly cooked vegetables, salads do not need to be 'dressed', particularly if fruit is an ingredient as this will often provide all the extra flavour and moisture that is necessary.

Indeed, oily dressings can be the undoing of the healthiness of light leafy salads, unless accompanied with lots of bread, rice or potatoes to balance the fats in the dressing.

If you are going to dress a salad, do this at the last minute, adding the oily component separately first. The oil will adhere to the salad ingredients and will help trap the watery juices so that they do not just sink to the bottom of the bowl. In the case of oil-free dressings it is better to let people dress their own portions at the table.

recipes

MANY BEAN SALAD

Serves 4

½ × 400g (14oz) can kidney beans, drained and rinsed
½ × 400g (14oz) can chick peas, drained and rinsed
60g (2oz) uncooked frozen peas, thawed
60g (2oz) French beans, trimmed, washed and cut in 1cm (½ inch) lengths
3 spring onions, trimmed and chopped
150ml (5oz) oil-based dressing

Place all the vegetables in a large serving bowl, add the dressing, and turn so that all the ingredients are well coated. Chill.

POTATO, APPLE AND BACON SALAD

Serves 4

340g (12oz) cooked new *or* waxy potatoes, cut into small chunks
1 red apple, washed, cored and chopped
140ml (¼ pint) Yogurt Dressing (see recipe, right)
a handful chives, chopped
4 slices crisply cooked bacon, chopped

Place the potatoes in a bowl. Mix the dressing with the chives, pour over the potatoes, and turn to coat them. Sprinkle with the bacon bits.

RICE SALAD

Serves 4

110g (4 oz) brown rice
2 teaspoons oil
60g (2oz) nut and raisin mixture
1 onion, peeled and chopped
60g (2oz) mushrooms, wiped and chopped
5cm (2 inch) length cucumber, washed and well chopped
8 spring onions, trimmed and sliced
8 radishes, washed and thinly sliced
handful chopped parsley
freshly ground black pepper

Place a generous quantity of water in a saucepan and bring to the boil. Add the rice, cover and boil for 30 minutes. Drain and turn the rice into a bowl.

Add the nuts and raisins to the hot rice. They will absorb some of the moisture and swell a little.

Place the oil in a non-stick frying pan, heat until it runs easily, then add the onion and sauté until soft. Add the mushrooms, and cook for ½ minute. Remove from the heat and mix into the rice. Fluff up with a fork. When cool, stir in the remaining ingredients.

YOGURT DRESSING

Makes 140ml (5 fl oz)

1 × 140ml (5fl oz) plain yogurt
2 teaspoons lemon juice, *or* to taste
freshly ground black pepper
Optional extra ingredients
1 *or* 2 teaspoons fruit purée *or* honey
1 clove garlic, crushed
2 teaspoons finely chopped onion
1 teaspoon curry powder *or* garam masala
1 handful watercress, finely chopped

Place the yogurt and lemon juice in a bowl, and whisk together with a fork. Season with pepper, then stir in any of the other optional ingredients.

OIL AND FRUIT JUICE DRESSING

Makes approx. 100ml (3½fl oz)

2 tablespoons oil (olive, grapeseed, corn, sunflower *or* soya)
1-2 tablespoons lemon juice
2 tablespoons orange, grapefruit *or* apple juice, *or* 2 tablespoons stock
freshly ground black pepper
Optional extra ingredients
crushed garlic to taste
1 tablespoon crushed walnuts
1 teaspoon chopped fresh herbs such as mint, coriander, *or* dill
1 teaspoon mild mustard

Above: *'Help Yourself'*
Vegetable Platter

recipes

Put the first 4 ingredients in a jam jar with a lid and shake vigorously until well mixed. If the dressing is too sharp for your taste substitute 1 tablespoon of apple juice or stock for 1 tablespoon lemon juice. Add in any of the optional ingredients and shake again.

'HELP YOURSELF' SALAD PLATTER

A platter or bowl of raw vegetables, where each vegetable is served separately so that children choose their own combination, is generally popular. This also gives an opportunity to introduce new items.

Salad platter: suggested ingredients
Sticks of carrot, celery, beetroot and courgette • french beans • thick chunks of cucumber • cherry *or* quartered tomatoes • split baby maizes • leek rings • segments of orange and grapefruit • slices of apple, banana and raw mushroom • radishes and spring onions • grapes • rings of red, yellow, and green pepper • sprigs of watercress and cress • onion rings • florets of cauliflower and broccoli
Salad bowl: excellent side salads can be made from a simple combination

of 2 or 3 ingredients, as follows:
leaves from 2 or 3 varieties of lettuce • grated swede and sultanas, dressed with orange juice • chunks of courgette and pineapple • torn spinach leaves and sliced mushrooms • tomato and onion rings with chives • shredded red cabbage, carrot and apple • avocado and pear • grated carrot, beetroot and lemon juice • kidney beans, diced carrot and chopped spring onion • diced pepper, sweetcorn and peas (thawed from frozen, but left uncooked) • tomato, apple and celery

Puddings

Most second courses nowadays consist of just a piece of fruit or yogurt. This is often sufficient and probably all that should be offered to children who might otherwise prefer not to fill up on the first course in order to leave extra room for the sweet pudding! Children who are growing fast or have large appetites, on the other hand, may well need something more substantial to fill them up. Cooked puddings or cakes are popular anyway, and if children are to be restrained from eating sweets and other sugary foods between meals, then there should be a time when such foods are permitted. Keeping sugary foods confined to mealtimes is a sensible solution.

Healthier puddings

Puddings can be perfectly healthy foods — what often makes them unhealthy is the topping used, such as fatty pastry or a generous layer of cream. A fruit pudding, for example, whether cooked or fresh, is a useful source of fibre and if cooked, can be made with a low-fat crumble or breadcrumb topping instead of pastry.

Although an occasional tablespoon of cream or icecream is unlikely to do much harm in an otherwise sensible diet, low-fat yogurt is better. This is not always liked, however, and the thicker Greek yogurt may be more acceptable: bear in mind, though, that if eaten in large quantities it will provide as much, if not more, fat than a smaller quantity of cream. There are many cream substitutes on the market which describe themselves as made with 'vegetable' fat but these descriptions are frequently misleading as the fat may still be as harmful as saturated fats, particularly when they are described as 'hydrogenated' on the label. Healthier, and just as tasty, are fruit purées and good old-fashioned custard, especially if it has been made with low-fat, rather than full-cream, milk.

Food values: TOPPINGS			
	protein	sugar	fat
cream, 1 tablespoon	.5g	.5g	3-7g
Greek yogurt, 2 tablespoons	4-6g	2-5g	4-9g
low-fat yogurt, plain 2 tablespoons	5g	7½g	1g
custard, 4 tablespoons	3g	9g	.5-3.5g
ice cream, 1 scoop	1.75g	11g	4g
dessert topping, 30g (1 oz)	1g	3g	3-4g

recipes

BANANA, RHUBARB AND ORANGE WHIP

Sweet banana and tart rhubarb complement each other well in this recipe.

Serves 3 – 4

3 – 4 sticks rhubarb, washed and chopped
140ml (5fl oz) orange juice
2 small ripe bananas, peeled and chopped
1 teaspoon coriander
caster sugar (see Method)

Place the rhubarb and orange juice in a saucepan, bring to the boil, reduce the heat, cover and simmer for about 5 minutes, or until soft. Place the rhubarb, and some of the cooking liquid, with the bananas and coriander, in a blender. Purée the fruit, adding extra cooking juice if necessary. (Alternatively, rub through a sieve.)

Taste to check the sweetness. You may need to add a little caster sugar if the bananas were not ripe enough.

Pour into serving dishes and chill.

BLACKCURRANT YOGURT WOBBLE

Serves 4

1 × 140g (5oz) tablet blackcurrant jelly
boiling water, to dissolve jelly
425ml (¾ pint) plain low-fat yogurt, extra as required (see Method)

Place the jelly tablet in a bowl and allow to dissolve in the minimum of boiling water, stirring occasionally. Allow the mixture to cool before making up to 550ml (1 pint) with the yogurt, mixing thoroughly. Pour into a mould or serving bowl and leave to set.

Variation Instead of the blackcurrant jelly, you can also make this with 1 × 12g (½oz) packet orange flavour, sugar-free jelly crystals. Dissolve in 250ml (scant ½ pint) boiling water, then add 3 tablespoons orange juice, and 275ml (½ pint) yogurt, as above.

CREAMY FRUIT SUNDAE

Here, sweet fruit and creamy yogurt make a lovely taste and texture.

Serves 6

225g (8 oz) mixed dried fruits such as apricots, peaches, pears and prunes
550ml (1 pint) tea
200g (7oz) thick plain *or* Greek yogurt
3 digestive biscuits, crushed

Pour the tea into a saucepan and bring to the boil. Add the fruit, reduce the heat and simmer for 10 minutes. Allow to cool, by which time the fruit should be soft and plump. Drain the fruit, reserving the cooking liquid for puréeing the fruit.

Stone the prunes, then process or blend the fruit with as much cooking liquid as will give you a thick, smooth purée. (Alternatively, rub through a sieve). Pour into glass tumblers.

Stir the yogurt, then spoon on top of the fruit purée in each tumbler. Finally add a spoonful of crushed digestives.

recipes

SLEEPY CHOCOLATE PEAR PUDDING

Sleepy is what you will feel after you have eaten this pudding!

Serves 6

110g (4oz) polyunsaturate margarine
110g (4oz) castor sugar
2 eggs, beaten
1 tablespoon milk
125g (4½ oz) wholemeal
self-raising flour
30g (1 oz) cocoa powder
1 kg (2lb) pears, peeled,
cored and chopped

Place all the ingredients, except the pears, in a blender and blend until smooth. Alternatively, cream together the margarine and sugar in a mixing bowl, mix in the eggs and milk, then fold in the flour and cocoa powder.

Place the chopped pears in the bottom of a 1.2 litre (2 pint) ovenproof dish. Pour over the cake mixture and bake in a preheated moderate oven, 180°C (350°F), Gas Mark 4, for 45 minutes.

Serve the pudding warm or cold, with chocolate custard, if liked (made in the usual way but with the addition of a little cocoa powder or melted chocolate for flavouring).

FRUIT CRUMBLE

Crumbles are easy, filling and popular.

Serves 4

450g (1lb) prepared fruit
(such as apples *or* pears, washed and cored,
or stoned plums *or* apricots)
sugar to taste, if the fruit is tart
4 – 6 tablespoons boiling water,
depending on firmness of the fruit
Crumble topping
100g (3½oz) wholemeal flour
30g (1oz) soft margarine
4 tablespoons rolled oats

Grease a 18cm (7 inch) ovenproof dish, and spread with the prepared fruit. Sprinkle with sugar and water as necessary, depending on the fruit used.

Place the flour in a bowl, add the margarine and rub into the flour with your fingertips or a knife (this stage can also be done in a food processor). Mix in the oats.

Spread the topping over the fruit, and bake in a preheated moderate oven, 180°C (350°F), Gas Mark 4, for 30 to 40 minutes, or until the topping is crunchy and golden brown.

Variation Instead of some of the oats you can also use sesame or sunflower seeds or flaked almonds in the crumble topping. You can also simply top fruit with oats on their own or with muesli.

*Above: Creamy
Fruit Sundae*

Teas and suppers

Most small children, who are tired at the end of the day, will only be able to manage a light meal for tea or supper. There can, however, be a surprising change in appetite when they start school. Older children naturally tend to be hungrier, and having a packed lunch or only partially eating their school dinner can make them feel ravenous on their return home. Some children are able to get by with a snack then, and wait for a more substantial meal in a couple of hours' time. Others are too hungry and, given the chance, will raid the kitchen for snacks leaving little room for a cooked meal later. For such children, changing meals around and serving a cooked meal soon after the return from school and, maybe, a snack later on may be the best solution.

recipes

Potatoes

Potatoes are probably the nearest there is to a 'complete' food. When eaten in sufficient quantity, they are an excellent source of good-quality protein, fibre, minerals and vitamins, and in particular Vitamin C, which is not found in other starchy foods like rice or bread.

Baked potatoes filled with foods like vegetables, beans, meat or fish make a very healthy base to a meal. Much of their goodness can be undone, though, if they are merely filled with large knobs of butter, margarine or sour cream, all fatty foods.

Chips, another popular way of serving potatoes, are less versatile, but certain varieties can still be healthy – for example, thick, oven chips made with corn or sunflower oil have half the fat of other sorts.

Choosing potatoes

There are several different varieties of potatoes, each suited to particular methods of cooking. Floury potatoes, like Maris Piper, are best mashed or baked, while yellow-fleshed or waxy potatoes like Pentland Javelin and 'new' potatoes are best boiled or used cold in salads. Good all-round varieties are Golden Wonder, King Edward and Desirée.

recipes

'STUFF YOUR OWN' BAKED POTATOES

Here the potato is the central ingredient of the dish and the fillings should be thought of as extras. Children love choosing their own fillings, so this is a particularly useful dish when other children come to tea and you are not sure of their likes and dislikes.

1 large (225g/8oz) baked potato per child (larger for adults, smaller for very young children)
Suggested fillings
Hot baked beans • red cabbage • buttered sweetcorn • hummus (see page 44) • bolognaise sauce • grated cheese • coleslaw • strips of ham • tuna mixed with low-fat mayonnaise • tatziki (chopped cucumber with yogurt)

Scrub and remove any blemishes. Prick the skin or, using a sharp knife, cut a cross on the top or score a line round the middle of the potato to release steam during cooking. To cook in a conventional oven, thread the potatoes on to skewers to speed the cooking process, and bake in the centre of a preheated moderately hot oven, 200°C (400°F), Gas Mark 6, for about ¾ to 1 hour. To test whether they are cooked press them with your fingers or pierce with a skewer: they should feel soft inside. Keep the potatoes in a warm place until ready to serve.

If cooking in a microwave, prick the skin in several places, wrap in kitchen paper (to prevent the skin becoming soggy), and microwave on Full for 3 to 6 minutes per potato, according to the manufacturer's instructions, with 5 minutes standing time. To crisp the skin, place the potatoes under a hot grill.

Arrange your chosen fillings in serving bowls or on plates and with some raw vegetable sticks, and let the children help themselves.

LATKES

These potato pancakes are tasty and will be appreciated by children who prefer eating with their fingers.
Makes 6
225g (8oz) grated raw potato
½ small onion, peeled and chopped
1 egg, beaten
1 rounded tablespoon flour
freshly ground black pepper
2 teaspoons oil

Place 2 or 3 pieces of kitchen paper in a colander and spread the potato over it. Cover with a plate, place a weight on top and leave for 10 minutes to drain.

Mix the potato with the onion and flour and gradually stir in the egg until the mixture forms a crunchy batter.

Heat the oil in a non-stick frying pan and, when hot, add spoonfuls of the mixture and flatten into rounds. Fry until golden on one side, then turn over to fry the other side. It will take about 20 minutes to fry all the latkes. They should be eaten almost straight away – but with a warning that they are hot!

BUBBLE AND SQUEAKY BACON

Heavenly and very satisfying – well worth cooking lots of extra vegetables so you can serve this the next day! The quantities given below are only a guide – use however much you like, or have available, of each vegetable, but remember that there must be enough potato to hold the mixture together.
Serves 1
1 – 2 slices of bacon
1 teaspoon oil (optional, see Method)
225g (8oz) cold, cooked potatoes
1 small onion, peeled and well chopped
leftover cabbage, chopped small

Place the bacon in a non-stick frying pan and dry-fry. Remove from the pan, chop into pieces, and keep warm. The fat left in the pan should be enough to cook the vegetables, but if the pan looks sticky add 1 teaspoon oil.

Mix the potato with the onion and cabbage and pile into the hot pan. Flatten with a spatula and leave to fry for about 5 to 10 minutes. Carefully turn over to brown the other side. The mixture will break up, but this does not matter. When the potato cake is as brown as you like it, carefully remove it from the pan and serve garnished with chopped bacon.

Storage

Potatoes have more flavour and keep best – particularly in frosty or humid conditions when they can easily rot – if they have a coating of earth to protect them. Although potatoes are often sold in plastic bags, they do not do well stored in these. If they have to be kept in plastic, the bag should have holes made in it to keep the potatoes well ventilated. It is also important to keep potatoes in a dark place, as light causes the build-up of the poison *solanine*. A sign of this is the green skin you sometimes see on potatoes, which is a concentrated source of the poison. (The green on carrots and other vegetables is harmless and can be left.)

Preparation and cooking

Potatoes do not need to be peeled, provided they are clean and any bad patches removed. Green skin should always be cut well away, as explained above. Whole potatoes are best steamed or microwaved.

Food values:
POTATOES and Convenience Foods

quantity	protein	fat
potato, large baked	5.25g	.25g
potato, small baked	2.5g	Trace
1 × 110g (4 oz) serving chips	4.25g	12g
1 serving oven chips	4.25g	7g
2 small sausages, grilled/fried	5.5g	10g
1 beefburger, fried	7.75g	6.5g
1 sausage roll	4g	20g
1 small tin spaghetti in sauce	3.5g	1.5g

Below: *'Stuff Your Own' Baked Potatoes with baked beans, tatziki, and sweetcorn*

Flans and pizzas

Flans are a useful way of making something out of small pieces of meat or vegetables. You can also speed preparation by making double quantities of pastry, and freezing one raw pastry shell for another occasion (rolling it out before freezing means that it will defrost more quickly).

Making good pastry

Pastry does not always have to be of a fatty type like shortcrust. It can also be made with potato or oatmeal though, like pizza doughs, these are better smoothed out with the fingers rather than rolled. Good pastry needs cool ingredients, as little water as possible, plenty of air in the mixture, the minimum of handling, a short period in a cool place so that the pastry can relax as the moisture spreads more evenly throughout, and baking at a high temperature. If using wholemeal flour, this tends to require more liquid. Using soft margarine or oil or mixing in a food processor can make it more difficult to produce a light airy texture compared with the rubbing-in method. However, a perfectly acceptable everyday pastry can be produced using wholemeal self-raising flour and smaller than usual quantities of polyunsaturate margarine.

Filling the pastry case

If you are using a sauce to fill a pastry case it does not have to be very thick to start with. When sauce mixtures cool below 93°C they thicken and, if too thick to begin with, they will congeal into a solid mass when cold. Filling the case with a warm sauce will help prevent the pastry from getting soggy.

Easy pizzas

A bread base — as used in pizzas — is even healthier than a pastry one. Commercial pizza mixes or the scone-type base described opposite are probably easiest. The toppings for these bases could not be simpler. All they require is a basic tomato layer using tinned or fresh tomatoes, a pinch of herbs and some cheese or a brushing of oil for the top. You can then put small quantities of almost anything you fancy in the middle.

recipes

BROCCOLI PIE

Makes one 20-23cm (8-9 inch) pie
2 dessertspoons oil
225g (8 oz) broccoli florets, washed and chopped
2 cloves garlic, peeled and chopped
1 rounded tablespoon flour
275ml (½ pint) vegetable stock
(*or* water mixed with ½ teaspoon vegetable extract)
pepper
225g (8 oz) cottage cheese
shortcrust pastry to cover a 20-23 cm (8-9 inch) flan dish
(see Pissaladière, page 46)
milk *or* beaten egg, to glaze (optional, see Method)

Roll out the pastry into a round large enough to cover a 20-23 cm (8-9 inch) flan tin, and set aside.

Place the oil in a non-stick saucepan, heat until it runs, then add the broccoli and garlic. Stir, cover with a lid and allow to sweat until the broccoli turns a bright green. Sprinkle with the flour and mix in.

Add the stock, bring to the boil, reduce the heat and simmer for 5 minutes. Remove from the heat and allow to cool a little. Sieve the cottage cheese and stir into the broccoli mixture. Pour this filling into the flan case.

Cover with the pastry lid, crimping the edge and cutting a slit in the top to allow steam to escape. Brush with milk or beaten egg, if liked, to glaze. Cook in a preheated hot oven, 200°C (400°F) Gas Mark 7, for 20 to 25 minutes, or until the pastry is golden brown.

Serve warm with new potatoes and a side salad of tomato and onion or orange and watercress.

TUNA AND BROAD BEAN FLAN

Makes one 20-23 cm (8-9 inch) flan
170-200g (6-7 oz) shortcrust pastry (see Pissaladière)
225g (8 oz) broad beans (frozen *or* fresh)
1 × 200g (7 oz) can tuna, well drained
75ml (⅔ pint) Low-fat White Sauce (see page 73)
onion rings, to decorate

Roll out the pastry and use to line a greased 20-23cm (8-9 inch) flan tin. Fill the raw pastry case with the beans and tuna, pour over the sauce and decorate with the onion rings.

Bake in a preheated fairly hot oven, 200°C (400°F), Gas Mark 6, for about 35 minutes. Serve warm or cold.

EGG AND MUSHROOM FLAN

Makes one 20-23cm (8-9 inch) flan
175-200g (6-7 oz) shortcrust pastry (see Pissaladière)
1 teaspoon oil
1 onion, peeled and chopped
80g (3 oz) mushrooms, wiped *or* peeled and sliced
2 eggs
220-275ml (8-10fl oz) milk
¼ teaspoon dried herbs
salt and pepper
a few strips ham *or* chopped cooked bacon (optional)
2 tomatoes, sliced

Line a flan dish with the pastry and prick the base. Place the oil in a non-stick

recipes

frying pan and heat until it runs easily.

Add the onion, stir and allow to soften with the lid on the pan for about 3 to 5 minutes, stirring occasionally. Add the mushrooms to the pan and allow to sweat for 3 to 4 minutes.

Beat the eggs with the milk, herbs and seasoning. Place the ham or bacon bits in the pastry case (if using) then add the onion and mushrooms. Pour over the egg and milk mixture and decorate with the sliced tomatoes.

Bake in a preheated fairly hot oven, 200°C (400°F) Gas Mark 6, for 35 to 45 minutes until the filling has set.

Below: Quick Pizza with cucumber wedges and thick oven chips

QUICK PIZZA

Pizza is a firm favourite with children. Here is a recipe which children could easily help to make. Not only is it quick to prepare, but it also tastes much nicer and is cheaper than bought pizzas.

Serves 4

225g (8 oz) self-raising flour
65g (2½ oz) soft margarine
milk to mix

Topping

1 large onion, peeled and sliced
3 *or* 4 large tomatoes, thinly sliced
½ teaspoon dried mixed herbs
strips of ham *or* some sliced raw mushrooms *or* green pepper rings
110g (4 oz) Cheddar *or* Mozzarella cheese, sliced

Place the flour in a mixing bowl, add the margarine and rub into the flour until the mixture resembles breadcrumbs. Add enough milk to make a soft but not sticky dough. (This can also be done in a food processor.) Roll out on a floured board into a circle about 1cm (½ inch) thick. Place on a greased baking tray.

Spread the remaining ingredients on top, finishing with the cheese. Bake in a preheated hot oven, 220°C (425°F) Gas Mark 7, for about 20 to 25 minutes.

Pasta

Pasta or noodles are fat-free, nutritious and have a moist, slippery texture which makes them easy to eat and a pleasant change from drier-tasting foods like flour, grains and potatoes. Pasta comes in many interesting shapes and even an assortment of colours, but it is all basically made from the same ingredients with few detectable variations in flavour or texture.

Fresh pasta needs to be kept in a fridge but takes only three minutes to cook and tastes better than dried pasta. It can also be frozen, and will then take only a couple of extra minutes to cook.

Sauces
Sauces for pasta can be simple purées of vegetables or nuts or they can be made from milk, stock or water which has been thickened with starch. When starch gets heated, the granules burst, making a gel, and it is this which sets the liquid. If the sauce is to be smooth it needs vigorous stirring. If using the all-in-one method of sauce making, in which all the ingredients are mixed together first, the liquid needs to be cold to start with and the mixture is then gradually heated. You can also mix the flour with some cold water, milk or stock and gradually add it to the hot cooking juices.

Flour and fat
Wholemeal flour is perfectly easy to use but gives a beige, flecked look to the sauce. Wheat flour gives a creamy texture but needs 10 minutes total cooking time to remove the 'raw' taste and to thicken properly. Cornflour cooks in less time but has a less interesting taste. Whichever flour you use will depend on which you find easiest and the nature of the other ingredients. Fat is really only necessary in sauces to help brown or caramelize flour. If wanted for flavour, you can use some other flavouring ingredient rather than fat.

Using a double boiler
Most sauces are best made — and certainly best reheated or kept hot — in a double boiler where one saucepan fits inside another, containing boiling water. This delays the drying out of the sauce as well as keeping a more even temperature which helps to avoid lumps. A double boiler is, of course, no use for browning the flour as the temperature never gets above boiling point.

recipes

MACARONI BAKE
Serves 4
250g (9 oz) macaroni or pasta shapes
1 teaspoon oil
1 medium onion, chopped
60g (2 oz) lean bacon, chopped
4-6 tomatoes, roughly chopped
550ml (1 pint) hot cheese sauce
(see Low-fat White Sauce, opposite)
grated cheese, to garnish

Bring a large saucepan of water to the boil, add the pasta and cook until *al dente* (just firm to the bite).

While the pasta is cooking, heat the oil in a non-stick saucepan. Add the chopped bacon and the onion, and allow to soften. Add the tomatoes and let the mixture simmer gently until the tomatoes are soft and the skins are peeling. Remove the skins if you wish. Pour into the bottom of a deep, greased, ovenproof dish, then spread the cooked pasta over the top.

Pour over the cheese sauce, sprinkle with a little extra cheese and place under the grill for a few minutes to brown.

Serve with raw vegetable sticks, such as celery or carrot, if liked.

VEGETABLE LASAGNE
This lasagne looks pretty and is a good opportunity to use up leftover sauces and vegetables. The fillings need to be fairly moist so that the lasagne can swell and cook properly.

Serves 4
1 × 200g (9 oz) pack no pre-cook lasagne verdi
30g (1 oz) grated cheese, for topping
Layer 1
3-4 leeks, puréed (see page 26)
Layer 2
450g (1 lb) spinach, washed, cooked, chopped and moistened with a little stock
Layer 3
275ml (½ pint) Tomato Sauce (see opposite)
Layer 4
275ml (½ pint) Low-fat White Sauce, or 275ml (½ pint) plain yogurt mixed with 70g (2½ oz) grated Wensleydale or Cheshire cheese

Pour the leek purée or spinach into the bottom of a greased ovenproof dish measuring about 23 × 23 cm (9 × 9 inches). Cover with a single layer of lasagne. Next, add the chopped spinach, then a layer of lasagne. Add the tomato sauce, followed by another layer of lasagne, finishing with a layer of white sauce or yogurt mixed with cheese.

Sprinkle with a little grated cheese and bake in the centre of a preheated fairly hot oven, 200°C (400°F), Gas Mark 6, for 35 to 40 minutes.

Variations Other good fillings are a Bolognaise sauce, fish in sauce, mushroom sauce, baked beans with chopped tomato, puréed fennel or broccoli or well-mashed swede moistened with milk or stock.

Above: Macaroni Bake with raw vegetable sticks

recipes

TOMATO SAUCE

Makes 275ml (½ pint)
1 teaspoon oil
1 small onion, finely chopped
1 clove garlic, crushed
250ml (9fl oz) sieved tomatoes
(½ carton/tin Passata) *or* 450g (1lb)
tomatoes with their green stalks,·
washed and quartered
1 bayleaf
½ teaspoon dried herbs

Heat the oil in a non-stick saucepan, then add the onion and garlic. Cover with a lid, turn down to a low heat and allow the onion to sweat for about 5 minutes or until it has softened.

Add the tomatoes and herbs, bring to the boil, reduce the heat, cover and simmer for a couple of minutes.

If using fresh tomatoes, cook with the lid on for about 10 minutes, or until the tomatoes are soft. Sieve to remove the skins, stalks and pips. Serve hot, mixed with pasta of your choice.

LOW-FAT WHITE SAUCE

This recipe for white sauce contains almost no fat and so is healthier than the usual variety. Low-fat skimmed milks have a tendency to burn, so cook in a double boiler or microwave.

Use in Lasagne or other baked pasta dishes, or mix with boiled pasta, and sprinkle with grated cheese. It can also be poured over vegetables, or used in baked vegetable dishes.

Makes 275ml (½ pint)
275ml (½ pint) skimmed milk
¼ medium onion
½ medium carrot
5cm (2 inch) celery, scrubbed
large bay leaf
6 peppercorns
1 tablespoon wholemeal *or* white
flour (heaped if you want a thick
sauce)
a little extra milk
pinch nutmeg
freshly ground black pepper

Place the milk, all but about 2 table-spoons, in a saucepan and bring to the boil with the vegetables, bay leaf and peppercorns. Remove from the heat and allow to infuse for at least 10 minutes. Strain and discard the infusion ingredients.

In a mixing bowl, combine the flour with the remaining cold milk to form a paste. Add the warm milk, stir well to make sure there are no lumps and return to the saucepan. Bring to the boil, reduce the heat and simmer until thick, stirring frequently. Cook for 10 minutes. Season with nutmeg and pepper.

Variations For a cheese sauce add 30g *(1 oz) grated mature Cheddar or mature Edam. Serve with extra grated cheese for a more cheesy flavour. For a herb-flavoured sauce, add a good handful of chopped fresh herbs such as parsley, dill or coriander. (These can be frozen in advance and saved for use in sauces.) For an egg sauce, add a well-chopped, hard-boiled egg.*

Soups and snacks

Children can be hungry anytime and soon discover that the fridge and the biscuit tin are happy hunting grounds for nibbles when they feel a bit 'peckish'. There are, however, some more healthy snacks you can offer.

Soups are warming and make an excellent winter snack. Something 'on toast' is also comforting. Remember, though, that snacks don't have to be cooked or hot: one of the most nourishing fillers is a chunk of plain bread or a roll.

Sugar between meals

Sugary foods like buns, biscuits and cakes should be avoided between meals, not only because they can spoil the appetite but also because of the risk to teeth — and 'sugar' does not just mean the refined, processed variety. Natural sugars can also be harmful to teeth when taken in dried fruit, honey or fruit juices where they are in a form which can coat the teeth (undiluted fruit juice contains the equivalent of 4 teaspoons of sugar per glass).

Suggested snacks

hot chocolate ● milk shakes made with fruit (see page 37) ● crispbreads or French toasts spread with a curd cheese, topped with fresh fruit ● rice cakes or crackers ● iced lollies made from fruit juices ● semi-frozen fruit yogurts ● savoury sandwiches ● a bowl of cereal with milk ● fruit and raw vegetables maybe with a dip (see page 46)

recipes

LENTIL SOUP

Lentils make some of the most nourishing and satisfying soups.

Serves 4

100g (3½ oz) red lentils, rinsed
2 teaspoons oil
1 onion, peeled and chopped
2 carrots, scraped and diced
550 ml (1 pint) stock
salt and freshly ground
black pepper (optional)
milk, for thinning

Place the lentils in a saucepan with enough water to cover and boil for 10 minutes. Drain. Heat the oil in the pan, add the onion and carrots, cover and allow the vegetables to sweat until the onion is soft, about 5 minutes.

Return the lentils to the pan. Add the stock and season if you wish. Cover, bring to the boil, reduce the heat and simmer gently for 45 minutes to 1 hour, or until the lentils are soft. Allow to cool and blend or press through a sieve. Thin with milk to the desired consistency, and adjust the seasoning. Serve hot.

LEEK AND POTATO SOUP

This is a quick soup to make and is lovely served with some really fresh bread.

Serves 6

1 tablespoon oil
4 large leeks, washed, lightly trimmed
and cut into thin rings
1 large potato, peeled
or scrubbed and chopped
820ml (1½ pints) stock
salt and freshly ground
black pepper (optional)
3-4 tablespoons milk (any variety)

Place the oil in a large saucepan and heat until it runs easily. Add the leeks and potato, cover and allow the vegetables to soften for 5 minutes.

Add the stock, bring to the boil, reduce the heat and simmer for about 30 minutes, or until the leeks and potato are soft and thoroughly cooked.

Purée the vegetables and cooking liquid in a blender, processing one third of the mixture at a time. Season to taste. Finally add the milk; this gives the soup an extra smoothness.

HOT BEETROOT SOUP

Choose the larger beetroot (about the size of a tennis ball) for this recipe, as the smaller ones will be too sweet.

Serves 4

340g (12 oz) raw beetroot, thinly
peeled and chopped
170g (6 oz) potato
peeled and chopped
1 large onion, peeled and finely
chopped
180ml (⅓ pint) orange
or tomato juice
370ml (⅔ pint) stock
4 tablespoons plain yogurt
140ml (¼ pint) milk (optional)
freshly ground black pepper
Garnish
chopped hard-boiled egg
chopped cold potatoes

Place the vegetables in a saucepan with the juice and stock. Bring to the boil, reduce the heat and simmer for 45 minutes. Purée the vegetables and cooking liquid in a blender, or pass through a sieve. Season with pepper. If liked, and add the milk if you prefer a thinner, blander soup.

Pour into individual bowls and drizzle one tablespoon of yogurt into each bowl. Serve with a side salad of chopped cold potato and hard-boiled egg.

EGGY BREAD

Serves 1

1-2 thick slices bread (depending on
whether sandwich or tin shape)
1 egg, well beaten with a pinch
cinnamon (optional)

Heat a non-stick frying pan until hot enough to melt a pea-sized lump of margarine, dropped into the pan.

Pour the egg into a wide dish or plate, and dip the bread into it. Place in the pan and cook on both sides.

recipes

TOASTIES

Here are some variations on the traditional 'cheese on toast'. Good cheeses for grilling are those like Cheddar, Edam and Gruyère. Thin slices are best (a hand-held cheese slicer, which is often part of a normal grater, is ideal for this).

Slices of wholemeal bread (quantity as required)
thin slices of cheese
Toppings
fresh apple rings, cored ● slices of tomato and onion rings, with a pinch of dried herbs
● slices of pepper and onion rings ● lightly sautéed, well chopped broccoli and onion

Place the bread under a hot grill and toast on one side only. Turn over and cover with any of the suggested toppings above. Finish off the 'toastie' by topping it with 2 or 3 slices of cheese.

Place under the grill again until the cheese bubbles, and serve.

MELBA TOAST

Melba toast will keep for several days in an airtight tin. Ready-sliced bread is moister than unsliced and so easier to use in this recipe.

Slices of bread (quantity as required)
Place several slices of bread under the grill, and toast on both sides. Pile the slices on top of each other and cut the crusts off. Then, with the palm of your hand on top, slice each piece through the soft middle and open out so that you now have two squares for each slice.

With the untoasted sides uppermost, pop back under the grill and toast. Watch carefully as they will curl up a bit and so can burn.

Below: Hot Beetroot Soup

Cakes and buns

The smell of baking is one of the most inviting smells there are and a home-made cake probably does more than any expensive food to make visitors feel welcome and special.

Fat content
Home-made cakes tend to be less sweet than shop-bought ones but many, particularly sponges, also tend to be fattier which is not so good. About the fattiest cake of all is a Victoria sponge with butter icing, where fat makes up one third of the cake's weight compared with less than one twentieth in the case of a jam Swiss roll. Fruit cakes are about halfway between the two extremes in fat content.

There are many other traditional recipes which are much less fatty than sponges, and if wholemeal flour is used their goodness can be even further improved without compromizing texture or flavour. Using wholemeal self-raising flour gives better results than adding baking powder to plain wholemeal flour, as it can be difficult to sieve the ingredients together thoroughly.

Why cakes rise
One of the principle differences between cake batters and pastry or biscuit mixtures is the addition of eggs. When fat and fine crystals of sugar are beaten together, air is trapped making the mixture light and fluffy. It is the presence of air and carbon dioxide gas produced by baking powder which causes the cake to rise. Once the cake has risen the air bubbles are then fixed in place by the hardening of the egg protein. This is why a cake may collapse if cold air from an open oven door is allowed to lower the temperature before the egg protein has set.

Preparation and cooking
Not all cakes need to have the fat and sugar creamed separately. Some recipes — particularly those using a food processor or mixer — can be made by mixing all the ingredients together at the same time. When baking it is particularly important to have the correct baking temperature and the right-sized tin — usually an 18 or 20 cm (7 or 8 inch) cake tin in the case of sponges and fruit cakes — or else the change in the thickness of the mixture will necessitate an alteration of the cooking time and maybe the temperature. It is easier to remove cakes from tins, whether non-stick or not, if they have first been lightly greased and lined with greased greaseproof paper. In the case of loaf tins a single strip of greaseproof paper running along the bottom and up both ends makes it easier to turn or lift out a cake.

Below: *Orange Yogurt Cake, Carrot Cake, Wholemeal Syrup Sponge Buns, Rock Buns*

recipes

ORANGE YOGURT CAKE

Makes one 450g (1 lb) loaf

110g (4 oz) margarine
80g (3 oz) caster sugar
½ teaspoon lemon zest
½ teaspoon orange zest
3 drops vanilla essence
2 eggs
140g (5 oz) self-raising flour, sieved with 1 teaspoon bicarbonate of soda
2 rounded tablespoons plain yogurt
Syrup
2 tablespoon orange juice
½ tablespoon lemon juice
1 tablespoon caster sugar

In a mixing bowl, cream together the margarine and sugar. Stir in the flavourings. Beat in the eggs, one at a time, with a little flour. Stir in the remaining flour and the soda, alternating with the yogurt, but do not beat at this stage. Spoon into a greased and lined 450g (1 lb) loaf tin, and bake in a preheated moderate oven, 180°C (350°F), Gas Mark 4, for 50 to 60 minutes.

Meanwhile make the syrup. Place the sugar and the juice in a saucepan, bring to the boil and boil for 2 to 3 minutes.

Turn the cake out of the tin, and pour the syrup over the top while still hot. You may need to make a few skewer holes in the cake to help the syrup to sink in.

Variation For a more elaborate cake you can spread lightly sweetened curd cheese or fromage frais *over the cake and decorate with mandarin slices.*

CARROT CAKE

This makes 2 loaves and freezes well.

Makes two 450g (1 lb) loaves

340g (12 oz) wholemeal
self-raising flour
1 teaspoon bicarbonate of soda
1 teaspoon mixed spice
225g (8 oz) granulated sugar
170ml (6fl oz) vegetable oil
2 teaspoons vanilla essence
3 eggs, beaten
110g (4 oz) grated carrot

1 × 375g (13 oz) tin crushed pineapple in natural juice, well drained
or 170g (6 oz) fresh pineapple
60g (2 oz) chopped walnuts (optional)

Grease two 450g (1 lb) loaf tins and line the base and both ends of each tin with a strip of greased greaseproof paper. It should be long enough to overhang the ends by about 5 cm (2 inches) on each side. Place the flour in a bowl and combine with the bicarbonate of soda, the mixed spice, and the sugar.

Make a well in the centre, pour in the oil, vanilla essence and egg, and beat well to form a smooth mixture. Fold in the carrot, pineapple and nuts and spoon the batter into the tins.

Bake in a preheated moderate oven, 180°C (350°F), Gas Mark 4, for 50 minutes. Turn the cake out on to a wire rack and leave to cool.

PARKIN

A useful cake which does not have to be made fresh to taste its best. In fact, it actually tastes better if made a day or two in advance to allow time for the flavour to develop. Store in a tin, or wrap in foil or cling film.

Makes one 20 × 20cm (8 × 8 inch) cake

340g (12 oz) medium oatmeal
110g (4 oz) wholemeal flour
60g (2 oz) brown sugar
½ teaspoon ground ginger
110g (4 oz) polyunsaturate margarine
110g (4 oz) black treacle
110g (4 oz) golden syrup
4 tablespoons milk
½ teaspoon bicarbonate of soda

Place the dry ingredients in a mixing bowl, and mix together. In a large saucepan, melt the margarine, treacle, and syrup together but do not allow the mixture to get too hot.

In another saucepan, warm the milk to blood heat (37°C), then stir in the soda. Pour into the treacle mixture, then stir in the dry ingredients and mix thoroughly.

Pour the batter into a lined and greased tin measuring about 20 × 20cm (8 × 8 inches). Bake in a preheated moderate oven, 180°C (350°F), Gas Mark 4, for about 1 hour, or until firm to the touch. Turn out on a wire rack to cool and, when cold, cut into squares.

ROCK BUNS

Makes 8

250g (9 oz) wholemeal
self-raising flour
pinch mixed spice
80g (3 oz) polyunsaturate margarine
60g (2 oz) sugar
1 egg
milk to mix (see Method)
110g (4 oz) currants

Place the flour in a mixing bowl, and add the spice. Rub in the margarine until the mixture resembles breadcrumbs. Add the sugar, egg, and the milk a tablespoonful at a time. The mixture should be fairly stiff. Finally add the currants, and stir thoroughly so that the fruit is evenly distributed through the batter.

Pile in 8 rough mounds on a baking tray lined with greased greaseproof paper, and bake in a preheated hot oven, 220°C (425°F), Gas Mark 7, for 15 to 20 minutes. Cool on a wire rack.

WHOLEMEAL SYRUP SPONGE BUNS

Makes 12 to 15

110g (4 oz) polyunsaturate margarine
80g (3 oz) caster sugar
30g (1 oz) golden syrup
2 medium eggs
140g (5 oz) wholemeal self-raising
flour

Add all the ingredients to a food processor and process for 30 seconds. Alternatively, beat together the margarine and sugar until light, then beat in the golden syrup. Add the eggs, stir thoroughly, then fold in the flour.

Spoon the mixture into sponge cases and bake in a preheated fairly hot oven, 190°C (375°F), Gas Mark 5, for 15 to 20 minutes. Cool on a wire rack.

Teabreads and biscuits

Children love making shapes with biscuit mixture. If biscuit shapes are to be cut, this should be done with a sharp cutting edge as a blunt knife or cutter will seal the edges making it difficult for the biscuit to rise properly. Cutters come in a variety of shapes or, if you want a particular shape, make a card template and cut around it. (If children are going to do any cutting, they should, of course, do this under supervision.)

When choosing biscuit recipes it is worth thinking about the proportions of fat, sugar and flour. Some biscuit mixtures are much fattier and sweeter than cakes whereas in other recipes, flour and/or oats are the principle ingredients. However if home-made biscuits are the only sweet biscuits in your home, it probably matters little what the recipe is as you are unlikely to have the time or inclination to make them in large quantities!

Types of biscuit

A biscuit dough is similar to pastry but with some extra flavouring ingredients added. Biscuits can be made short and crumbly with fast cooking at high temperatures; made crisper with more fat and sugar and slow baking; made crunchy with the addition of oatmeal or nuts; or made harder and more brittle like gingernuts using a melted-fat method. Whether the ingredients are creamed or rubbed together

recipes

BANANA LOAF

This recipe provides an excellent way of using up overripe bananas. Like most teabreads, this can be served plain, without spreading it with butter or margarine in the traditional way.

Makes one 450g (1 lb) loaf
80g (3 oz) polyunsaturate margarine
80g (3 oz) caster *or* brown sugar
1 egg, beaten
225g (8 oz) self-raising flour
¼ teaspoon bicarbonate of soda
2 ripe bananas, mashed
handful broken walnuts (optional)
milk (optional, see Method)

Place all the ingredients, except the walnuts (if using) and the milk, in a food processor, and blend until smooth. Fold in the walnuts.

If you are not using a processor, place the margarine and sugar in a mixing bowl and cream together until light. Beat in the egg with a little of the flour. Work in the remaining ingredients, except the milk, until well blended.

If the bananas do not moisten the mixture sufficiently, add a little milk until the batter is able to drop from a spoon.

Pour into a lined and greased 450g (1 lb) loaf tin and bake in the middle of a preheated moderate oven, 180°C (350°F), Gas Mark 4, for 1 hour.

Turn the loaf out on to a wire rack and leave to cool.

TEA LOAF

Makes one 450g (1 lb) loaf
225g (8 oz) raisins and sultanas
30g (1 oz) candied peel (optional)
420ml (¾ pint) tea
2 slices lemon
225g (8 oz) wholemeal
self-raising flour
60g (2 oz) granulated sugar
1 teaspoon mixed spice

Place the fruit in a saucepan with the lemon slices and tea, bring to the boil, reduce the heat and simmer for 5 minutes. Leave the fruit to cool and soak for at least 30 minutes. Remove the lemon slices and drain the fruit, reserving the cooking liquid.

Place the dry ingredients in a mixing bowl and stir in the fruit and sufficient cooking liquid to make a moist dough.

Scoop into a lined and greased 450g (1 lb) loaf tin and bake in the middle of a preheated moderate oven, 180°C (350°F), Gas Mark 4, for 1 to 1¼ hours, or until golden brown. Turn out on to a wire rack to cool.

OAT CRUNCHIES

Makes 20 to 25
60g (2 oz) polyunsaturate margarine
60g (2 oz) sugar
110g (4 oz) wholemeal self-raising flour
110g (4 oz) rolled oats

140ml (5fl oz) milk
½ teaspoon vanilla essence

In a mixing bowl, cream together the fat and sugar. Beat in the flour and oats, then add the milk and stir to blend.

Spoon dollops of the mixture on to a baking tray lined with greaseproof paper, and flatten a little. Bake in a preheated fairly hot oven, 190°C (375°F), Gas Mark 5, for 20 minutes. Leave to cool on the tray for a short time, then carefully remove to avoid breaking.

DROP SCONES

These are excellent eaten plain, straight from the pan, or with reduced-sugar jam.

Makes 15
110g (4 oz) wholemeal
self-raising flour
30g (1 oz) caster sugar
1 egg
140ml (5fl oz) milk
1 tablespoon plain yogurt
oil for greasing pan (see Method)

Place all the ingredients in a food processor and blend to form a thick batter. Alternatively, place the flour and caster sugar in a mixing bowl and mix together. Make a well in the centre, pour in the remaining ingredients and work into the flour, beating to remove any lumps.

Brush a non-stick frying pan with a tiny amount of oil, and heat. When the pan is hot, pour in dessertspoonfuls of the

can also affect the texture. Beating the mixture so that more air is trapped results in a more cake-like texture, whereas mixing the ingredients slowly results in a stiffer, denser biscuit.

Low-fat teabreads

Teabreads or fruit loaves are often made without any fat and most, if not all, their sweetness and moisture comes from dried fruit, especially if the fruit has been soaked beforehand.

batter. Wait for the mixture to set and for bubbles to appear on the surface, then turn over and cook the scones on the other side until brown.

Remove from the pan and keep moist in a clean napkin while you cook the remaining scones.

JUMBLES

Makes 16 to 20

110g (4 oz) margarine
110g (4 oz) caster sugar
1 small egg
225g (8 oz) wholemeal flour
1 teaspoon grated lemon zest
or ¼ teaspoon cinnamon and
60g (2 oz) currants *or* 1 tablespoon
cocoa powder

In a mixing bowl cream the margarine with the sugar until light. Beat in the egg with some of the flour. Stir in the flour and flavouring and knead lightly until the mixture forms a smooth ball.

Break off walnut-sized pieces of the mixture and place on a baking tray lined with greaseproof paper. Flatten with a fork dipped in hot water. Alternatively, roll the dough out between two sheets of greaseproof paper, prick with a fork and cut into rings.

Bake in a preheated moderate oven, 180°C (350°F), Gas Mark 4, for about 15 to 20 minutes. Allow to cool briefly on the tray, then remove.

Below: Drop Scones, Tea Loaf, Oat Crunchies, Jumbles

Special occasions

Special occasions are times when the rules of everyday eating are often relaxed a bit. The food may be a bit more exotic or unusual and children may be allowed to leave the table between courses so that the adults can talk with fewer interruptions.

In the case of young children, changing the usual routines can be upsetting. Late meals make for hungry, cross children and suddenly being expected to behave 'better' because an older relative is coming may simply result in a mutinous toddler. The occasion may be made more harmonious if babies and toddlers are given their meal first so that hunger and any mess can be dealt with beforehand. Older, but still young, children can be given one end of the table to themselves, away from the interruptions of adults!

Sunday lunches

Sunday lunch — the roast joint of meat or poultry with gravy or a sauce and vegetables, followed by a pudding — is a tradition that is still honoured despite, or maybe because of, the increasing informality of other meals.

The Sunday 'roast' is actually a misnomer. Only large hunks of meat which are turned on an open spit and basted with fat to prevent them drying out during a lengthy cooking process are truly 'roasted'. Small joints, cooked in an enclosed space like an oven, cook much more speedily, and this method is really baking, not roasting.

Dry roasting
Virtually all meats have enough of their own fat not to need any extra added for cooking. Some fat can even be completely removed, such as the lumps often found inside the opening of the body cavity of a chicken.

If meat such as a large turkey has to be cooked for a long period then the skin will need to be protected with foil for most of the cooking time. Otherwise, simply place the piece of meat in a pan, or on a rack if you want to baste it, and make sure the oven is at the correct temperature before putting in the meat. This method not only browns the meat but allows fat to drain off.

Joints with bones tend to cook quicker than unboned joints. This is because the bone conducts heat to the centre, speeding up the cooking process.

Allow the meat to stand for 15 minutes on a clean dish before carving, but not in the roasting tin containing the run-off fat. During this time the meat will become more succulent.

Although at first the meat juices run out, as the hot meat continues to cook it reabsorbs these juices. This process may be upset if the bottom is burnt or if too much fat is present, acting as a barrier to reabsorption.

Carving
Carving with a sharp knife also keeps meat juicy as a blunt knife squashes the meat fibres, so squeezing out their juices.

Slow cooking
Pot-roasting, in which a small amount of liquid is used to braise cheaper, tougher cuts like silverside of beef, is a practical alternative to the traditional 'roast'. It enables large pieces of meat to be cooked for long periods, leaving the cook free to get on with other parts of the meal in the meantime.

recipes

CHICKEN IN THE POT
A virtually foolproof, flavoursome dish for those Sundays when it is going to be difficult to time meals exactly. This dish can take as little as half an hour to cook using a ready-made stock, and can safely be left in the hot stock until you are ready to serve. It also incidentally produces a good stock which you can use in other dishes, such as soups or casseroles.

Serves 4-6

1.2 litres (2 pints) cold water
1 onion, peeled
1 carrot, scraped and chopped in half,
or 1 leaf lovage
1 clove garlic (unpeeled)
9 peppercorns
1 bouquet garni
1 chicken, weighing about
1.5 kg (3½ lb)

Place all the ingredients except the chicken in a large casserole. Bring to the boil, cover, reduce the heat and gently simmer for about ½ to 1 hour.

Remove any fat from inside the chicken and add the chicken to the hot stock. Continue to simmer gently as before for a further 20 minutes.

Remove from the heat. Take out the chicken and set aside. Spoon out the vegetables, giblets and bouquet garni and discard. Skim the stock. Return the chicken to the casserole.

Carve the meat, discarding the skin, and arrange on a serving dish with a little stock poured over it to keep it moist. The remaining stock should be cooled and the fat removed.

CRISPY DRY ROAST POTATOES
This recipe uses less fat than in traditional roast potatoes.

medium potatoes (quantity as
required) peeled and quartered
1 tablespoon oil for a small roasting
pan, 2-3 tablespoons for a large pan

Place the potatoes in a saucepan, cover with water, bring to the boil and cook for 15 minutes. Drain thoroughly.

Pour the oil into the roasting pan and heat for a couple of minutes on the top shelf of a preheated hot oven, 220°C (425°F) Gas Mark 7. Tip the pan about so that the oil covers the base.

Add the potatoes to the tin and cook for about 30 to 45 minutes or until the tops are nicely browned.

BROWN GRAVY SAUCE
Gravy made from meat juices tends to be very fatty. This is a low-fat version which has the added advantage that it can be made in advance rather than waiting until the last moment while the meat is standing.

Makes 275ml (½ pint)

2 teaspoons oil
1 small carrot, scraped
and finely chopped

Above: Chicken in the Pot with Brown Gravy Sauce, Crispy Dry Roast Potatoes, and vegetables

recipes

1 onion, peeled and very finely chopped
275ml (½ pint) stock, *or* water mixed with ½ teaspoon vegetable extract *or* ¼ vegetable stock cube
1 tablespoon flour for a thick gravy, ½ tablespoon for a thinner sauce

Place the oil in a non-stick frying pan and heat until it runs easily. Add the vegetables and fry until they begin to brown, to add flavour. Add the flour, stir and brown for 3 minutes or so — this is important as it again adds flavour.

Add about 1 tablespoon of stock and stir thoroughly to make a very thick paste. Add half the remaining liquid, stirring thoroughly, then pour in the remaining liquid, stirring again to make sure there are no flour lumps. Bring to the boil, and simmer for 8 to 10 minutes, to thicken the gravy.

Strain before serving, if you prefer a smoother sauce.

NUTTY PLUM TART

This delicious pudding is excellent for Sunday lunch or for entertaining.

Makes one 20cm (8 inch) tart

Pastry
70g (2½ oz) medium *or* fine oatmeal
110g (4 oz) wholemeal self-raising flour
70g (2½ oz) polyunsaturate margarine
1½ tablespoon cold water

Filling
60g (2 oz) sponge cake crumbs, *or* 1 egg yolk, beaten
560g (1¼ lb) plums, stoned and halved
60g (2 oz) caster sugar
1 level teaspoon cinnamon
60g (2 oz) flaked almonds

First make the pastry. In a mixing bowl, combine the oatmeal and flour. Rub in the margarine until the mixture resembles breadcrumbs, letting it run through your fingers so that it stays well aerated.

Add the water and mix quickly to bind the ingredients and form a firm dough.

This mixture is very crumbly, so it needs a slightly different technique from the usual shortcrust dough. Roll it out into a thick circle and transfer to a lightly greased 20cm (8 inch) tin. With your fingers, work out the dough to the edges of the tin and up the sides. Prick the base. In order to prevent the pastry becoming soggy from the fruit, either sprinkle the pastry base with sponge cake crumbs or brush the base with the beaten egg yolk.

Arrange the plum halves over the base, sprinkle with the sugar and cinnamon and finally the flaked almonds. Bake in a preheated fairly hot oven, 200°C (400°F), Gas Mark 6, for 20 minutes. Then reduce the heat to 180°C (350°F), Gas Mark 4, and cook for a further 10 to 15 minutes. The sugar gives a pleasantly frosted look. Eat warm or cold.

Family entertaining

When entertaining other families, the occasion is likely to be much more successful if food preparation is kept simple and if you make sure in advance that at least some of the food offered will be familiar to the visiting children. If they are kept happy, then the adults will be better able to enjoy themselves too! Alternatively, if you do not know what the children will like, a basket of bread and some salad vegetables on the table and a selection of a few cold meats or cheeses ready to hand should provide even the most timid eater with something to choose.

Safe cooking in advance

Special care has to be taken when cooking large quantities of food in order to avoid food poisoning, especially if the food has to be cooked in advance. Large casseroles or pans of soup take much longer to cook and to reheat, thus providing conditions which encourage bacteria to grow. It is therefore best to divide the recipe quantity between two or more dishes so that the food cools quicker. Large quantities will take up much less space in the fridge or freezer if they are stored and stacked in plastic boxes, such as clean ice cream containers. Rice, a common source of bacterial contamination, can be cooled down quickly by running under cold water — which will also help prevent the grains sticking.

Reheating

When reheating casseroles and soups it is important to stir the dish or pan thoroughly from time to time so that all the contents are heated thoroughly and evenly. After a large party, when cooked food has been left at room temperature for longer than the recommended 1½ hours, it is safest to throw it away.

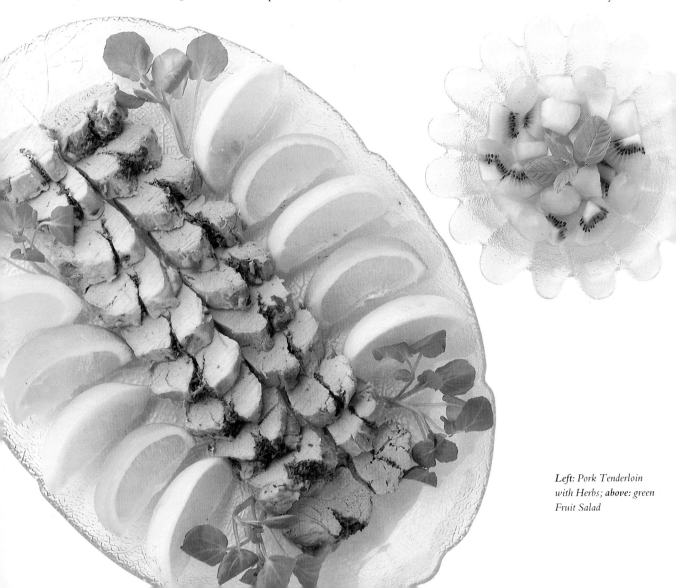

Left: Pork Tenderloin
with Herbs; *above:* green
Fruit Salad

recipes

ORIENTAL LAMB CASSEROLE

This recipe for lamb is spicy without being as hot as a curry.

Serves 8

900 g (2 lb) lean lamb (such as leg or shoulder), cubed
2 large onions, peeled and chopped
2 cloves garlic, peeled and chopped
2 tablespoons tomato purée
2 teaspoons ground ginger
1 teaspoon ground nutmeg
1 teaspoon cumin seed
550 ml (1 pint) stock
60 g (2 oz) raisins (optional)
60 g (2 oz) mushrooms, washed and quartered
2 level dessertspoons cornflour (optional)

Place the meat in a non-stick frying pan and allow to brown for about 10 to 15 minutes (lamb provides enough of its own fat not to need any extra for cooking). During cooking, drain off any fat that runs from the lamb.

Add the onions and garlic to the pan and allow to soften. Add the tomato purée and the ginger, nutmeg and cumin seed and cook for 1 minute. Stir in the stock, raisins and mushrooms.

Spoon the mixture into an ovenproof dish, cover, and bake in a preheated moderate oven, 180°C (350°F), Gas Mark 4, for 1 to 1¼ hours. For a thicker sauce, mix the cornflour with a little cold water and stir into the casserole 5 minutes before the end of cooking.

PORK TENDERLOIN WITH HERBS

Served in slices and garnished with orange and lemon wedges, this makes a very attractive dish.

Serves 4

675 g (1½ lb) pork fillet, in one or two pieces
1-2 very small knobs margarine
30 g (1 oz) well-chopped mixed fresh herbs (such as parsley, dill, marjoram, coriander)
juice of 2 cloves of garlic
juice of 2 cubes of root ginger (optional)
lemon juice

Garnish

4 lemon wedges
4 orange wedges
watercress

Slice the fillet lengthwise about three-quarters of the way through to open it out. Spread the inside with a tiny knob of margarine, then spread the herbs over this. Squeeze the garlic juice, ginger juice, if used, and some lemon juice over the meat. Roll the fillet back to its original shape and, if necessary, skewer each end with a cocktail stick to keep it closed. Place the fillets in an ovenproof dish and sprinkle with a little more lemon juice. Place the dish in a roasting bag, seal, and leave the meat to marinate for half an hour (or it can stay for several hours in the fridge.)

Bake in a preheated moderate oven, 180°C (350°F), Gas Mark 4 for 25 to 30 minutes. Serve sliced into 2 cm (¾ inch) rounds, garnished with the lemon and orange wedges and the watercress. The juice from the fruit provides a dressing for the meat.

SUMMER PUDDING

This can be made from many soft fruits, not just the traditional summer berries. Blackberry and apple is good and bottled blackcurrants are a year-round standby. A total of 900 g (2 lb) fruit is needed for a 820 ml (1½ pint) bowl.

Serves 6-8

6-7 thin slices wholemeal bread with crusts removed
450 g (1 lb) fresh blackcurrants *or*
675 g (1½ lb) bottled blackcurrants
4 kiwi fruit, peeled and chopped

If you are using fresh blackcurrants, stew the fruit briefly with 140 ml (5 fl oz) water and sugar to taste.

Line an 820 ml (1½ pint) pudding bowl with the bread. Drain the blackcurrants, reserving the cooking syrup or juice. Add the kiwi fruit and 2 tablespoons of syrup or juice. Place a piece of bread on top. Add the drained blackcurrants and another 2 tablespoons juice. Cover with bread, making sure there are no gaps.

Place a saucer on top of the pudding and press down to squeeze juice into the bread. Remove the saucer and add more juice as necessary to colour the bread lightly (don't be tempted to use too much juice, as this will make the pudding collapse). Replace the saucer, add a heavy weight like a jar of jam, and chill for a few hours.

Just before serving, remove the saucer and run a palette knife gently round the inside of the bowl to help release the pudding. Invert the bowl over a plate and, keeping a firm hold on plate and bowl, shake to release the pudding.

Gently remove the bowl. Serve with thick, Greek yogurt.

FRUIT SALAD QUARTET

Putting together a fruit salad in one colour can look very striking. A scattering of mint sprigs makes a pretty decoration. The following fruit combinations look and taste good, but you can use whichever combinations you like, depending on cost and what is in season.

Black fruit salad
pitted black cherries, halved and deseeded black grapes, and blackberries, dressed with blackcurrant juice

Red fruit salad
strawberries, raspberries and chunks of deseeded water melon, dressed with red grape juice

Green fruit salad
halved seedless grapes, peeled and sliced kiwi fruit and chunks of honeydew melon, dressed with apple juice

Yellow fruit salad
slices of peach, mango and chunks of cantaloup melon, dressed with apple *or* orange juice

Birthday parties

Small children usually have only small appetites for party food, especially at teatime. From the age of five, though, most children's appetites can be quite hearty. Familiar foods like crisps or pizza squares will be appreciated most, but serve the more nourishing savoury items before the sweet foods, or little savoury food will be eaten.

Decorating the table

It is worth listening to your children's suggestions for decorating the table and presenting the food and, even better, giving them tasks to do as well as things to make so that they can really feel it is *their* party and not yours! For example, they could write out name places and decorate plain paper plates with wax crayons or non-toxic colour pens. A simple white, ironed sheet will make an effective background tablecloth for coloured plates and foods.

The birthday cake

As far as the cake is concerned, simple shapes are the most effective: a round shape can be turned into a clown's face and decorated with a paper hat, or a string of buns can be transformed into a caterpillar or snake, for example. What would be even more popular is letting your child decorate his own cake with silver balls, chocolate buttons and hundred and thousands, and even 'painting' a picture on some plain icing with food colouring and a clean paintbrush.

Other ideas

Tiny bridge rolls can be spread with savoury toppings and transformed into 'boats' with cocktail stick 'masts' and paper 'sails'. Bowls of vegetable sticks or small fruits are often popular and refreshing. Jelly is popular, too, and can be made more interesting if set in an animal-shaped mould or scooped-out orange halves; different coloured layers also look attractive. (Make sure each layer is set before adding the next *cooled* quantity.) You can also make 'hedgehogs' using a long bread roll spiked with cocktail sticks bearing sausages or cubes of cheese and pineapple, with raisins for eyes and a grape for the nose. 'Hot Dogs' are good for a winter party, and plain popcorn makes a healthier alternative to crisps.

Cleanliness

Lining up the children to have their hands washed before and after the food can also help calm down little people, as well as maintaining general cleanliness.

Right: a selection of quick and easy foods to serve at a child's birthday party, with the clown birthday cake taking pride of place

recipes

BASIC SPONGE

A slightly less sweet version of the usual Victoria sponge cake mix.

Makes one 18 cm (7 inch) sandwich

170 g (6 oz) caster sugar
170 g (6 oz) soft margarine
3 eggs
200 g (7 oz) self-raising flour
Optional flavourings
1 heaped tablespoon cocoa powder, *or* zest of 1 lemon and/*or* orange, *or* a few drops vanilla essence, *or* 2 teaspoons instant coffee powder, dissolved in 1 teaspoon boiling water

In a mixing bowl, cream together the sugar and margarine until light. Add the eggs one at a time, with a little flour. Beat in thoroughly and stir in any flavouring agent which is being used. Add the remaining flour and beat well.

Pour into 2 greased and lined 18 cm (7 inch) sandwich tins and bake in a preheated moderate oven, 190°C (375°F), Gas Mark 5, for 20 to 30 minutes, or until the cakes spring back lightly when touched. The mixture can also be baked in a square 20 × 20 cm (8 × 8 inch) tin, in which case you should lower the oven temperature to 160°C (325°F), Gas Mark 3, and increase the cooking time to 35 to 40 minutes.

Allow the cakes to cool slightly in the tins, then turn out on to a wire rack to cool completely.

Sandwich the cakes together with reduced-sugar jam, or top with curd cheese or Fruit Curd (see page 35) or use either of the fillings that follow.

CHOCOLATE YOGURT FILLING

Fills or tops one 18 cm (7 inch) sandwich

60 g (2 oz) plain chocolate
140 ml (5 fl oz) thick plain yogurt

Place the chocolate in a bowl over a saucepan of hot water, and allow to melt. Stir in the yogurt, and chill. As the chocolate cools, it thickens the yogurt so that it can be spread on the sponge.

VANILLA CREAM FILLING

This filling is particularly good in a chocolate cake in which one half of the sponge is spread with the cream and the other with reduced-sugar blackcurrant jam.

Fills one 18 cm (7 inch) sandwich

60 g (2 oz) polyunsaturate margarine
60 g (2 oz) caster sugar
4 teaspoons hot water
6 teaspoons cold milk
2 drops vanilla essence

In a mixing bowl, cream together the margarine and sugar. Then beat in the hot water, 1 teaspoonful at a time.

Stir the vanilla essence into the milk, and add to the margarine and sugar mixture in the same way as the water. Adding the cold liquids gradually helps to firm the mixture whilst keeping it fluffy.

Barbecues

Barbecues are generally popular with children because there is plenty of opportunity for them to help, keeping an eye on how the food is cooking — they should of course never be left alone with a barbecue, without an adult there to supervize. Barbecues also mean eating with fingers and eating outdoors — both activities which children usually love.

Two disadvantages of barbecues, however, are that the charcoal can take a long time to heat up so that the start of cooking is delayed and large quantities of food may take some time to cook. To allow for this, a bit of pre-planning and even a bit of 'cheating' like part-cooking some meat in the oven may be called for!

Equipment
Barbecue grills do not have to be costly. Probably more versatile, and certainly cheaper than a large barbecue, is to have two, or even three small portable ones. They can cope with a surprisingly large amount of food and can easily be moved about.

Chops, sausages and chicken pieces can be put straight on to the barbecue grill. In the case of kebabs, the meat and vegetables should be threaded on to long, flat metal skewers so they can be turned easily. Hamburgers, stuffed pitta breads and fish, particularly if they are a bit fragile, are much easier to deal with if they are sandwiched between two wire grills with handles. You can get special shaped ones for fish. Finally, you will need a pair of long-handled tongs for turning food over.

Safe barbecuing
Barbecuing over open coals produces a much more intense heat than even that produced by a hot oven. These very high temperatures 'brown' the meat much more, so producing very intense flavours. However, because the outside can blacken quickly the inside may still be raw and cold. This may not be a hazard in the case of solid lumps of meat like steaks, where the inside muscle fibres are relatively free of dangerous bacteria, but it is a risk with meat products like sausages and hamburgers, where the inner meat has been mixed with surface bacteria. For this reason, hamburgers and the like should never be served 'rare', and will cook quicker and more safely if they are thin rather than thick. Learning to judge the right distance you should keep between the food and the fire, so that the inside is cooked by the time the outside is a pleasant dark brown, is a skill which has to be learnt with experience.

Marinating
Marinating meats can add to the flavour and marinating certain vegetables is essential if they are to be moist. If you want to baste food with some marinade during cooking, remember to reserve some for basting before adding to the raw ingredients. It is important not to use any which has been in contact with raw food, especially raw meat, otherwise you risk contaminating cooked food with bacteria. For the same reason, meat, once it is barbecued, should be put on a clean plate, never back in the dish which held the raw meat.

recipes

FISH KEBABS
Firm-fleshed fish need to be used for this such as monkfish or cod.
Serves 6
1.25 kg (2½ lb) fish, cut into chunks
2 medium red *or* green peppers, each cut into 6 pieces
1 bulb fennel, cut into 6 lengthwise
12 bay leaves
140 ml (5 fl oz) marinade (see Barbecue Marinade)
Place the fish in a bowl with the marinade (reserving some for basting), and marinate for 20 to 30 minutes. Thread on to skewers, alternating with the red or green peppers, fennel and bay leaves. Baste with the remaining marinade while cooking.

VEGETABLE KEBABS
Serves 6
2 teaspoons oil
1 small aubergine, cut into 12 chunks
3 medium onions, peeled and quartered
12 small tomatoes
24 good-sized mushrooms, cleaned and wiped
2 medium red or green peppers, each cut into 6 pieces
1-2 packs smoked tofu, chopped into 1 inch cubes
140 ml (5 fl oz) marinade (see Barbecue Marinade)
Heat the oil in a non-stick frying pan and dry-fry the aubergine. Marinate with the mushrooms, peppers and tofu for a couple of hours. Thread all the ingredients alternately on to skewers and baste them with the remaining marinade as they barbecue.

HOMEMADE HAMBURGERS
Serves 4
450 g (1 lb) mince
½ onion, finely chopped
freshly ground black pepper
pinch mixed herbs (optional)
oil, for brushing burgers (optional, see Method)

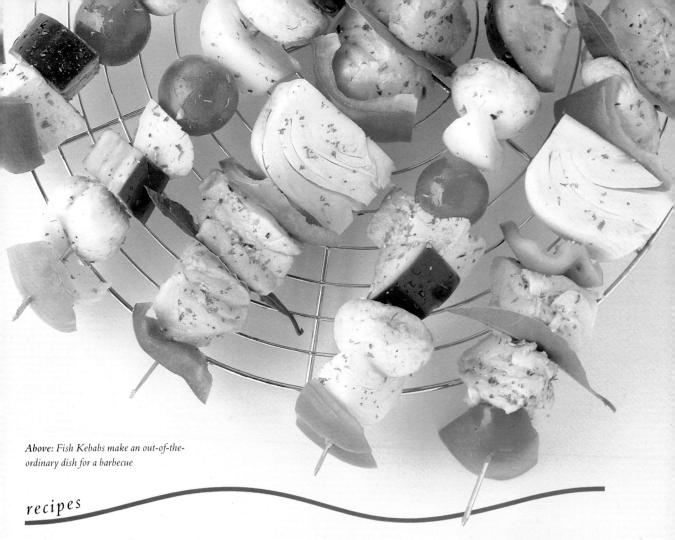

Above: Fish Kebabs make an out-of-the-ordinary dish for a barbecue

recipes

As there is nothing to bind the meat, the meat needs to be finely ground or else the hamburgers fall to pieces. Grinding meat also tenderizes it, which is why burgers need only a short cooking time.

Place the mince, onion, pepper, and herbs, if using, in a food processor, and process until you have a well-blended mixture (or place in a mixing bowl and grind with a pestle).

Shape the mixture into 4 large or 8 smaller balls and flatten to form rounds 5 mm – 1 cm (¼ – ½ inch) thick. Cook over the barbecue (or under the grill). If the meat is very lean you may need to brush the burgers with oil before you cook them to prevent burning.

CHICKEN DRUMSTICKS IN BARBECUE SAUCE

Serves 4
8 chicken drumsticks
Sauce
1 medium onion, peeled and finely chopped
1 clove garlic, crushed
½ x 400 g (14 oz) tin tomatoes, well chopped
1 tablespoon lemon juice
1 tablespoon soy sauce *or* Worcester sauce
2 teaspoons brown sugar
2 teaspoons oil
freshly ground black pepper

In a mixing bowl, combine all the ingredients for the sauce. Wipe the chicken, coat with the sauce (reserving some for basting) and leave to marinate for 20 minutes or more. (If baking in the oven remove the chicken skins before marinating — see below.)

Barbecue the chicken, basting it with the reserved sauce as it cooks. Alternatively, you can cook the chicken in the conventional way by baking it in a preheated oven, 220°C (425°F), Gas Mark 7, for 30 minutes.

Check that the drumsticks are cooked by inserting a skewer into the flesh: the juices should be clear.

BARBECUE MARINADE

Marinades are really used to add flavour. Wine, beer, lemon juice, vinegar, pineapple juice and tomato juice will also help tenderize meat, but they need heat to do this and so only have an effect with slow cooking. Meat or fish dishes need marinating for only 20 to 30 minutes; vegetables can be given longer. You can use your favourite dressing as a marinade (oil-based for vegetables or it will not adhere) or try the recipe below.

Makes 140 ml (5 fl oz)
1 teaspoon brown *or* caster sugar
4 tablespoons olive *or* grapeseed oil
3 tablespoons wine vinegar
2 tablespoons red wine
¼ teaspoon made mustard
¼ teaspoon mixed herbs
½ teaspoon freshly squeezed root ginger juice
salt and freshly ground black pepper

Place all the ingredients in a jam jar. Close with a lid and shake.

Christmas

Christmas may be a time of year when most people decide to blow caution to the winds and indulge themselves with whatever they fancy to eat. Ironically much of the traditional fare is actually low in fat and rich in fibre and other nutrients. Turkey is a naturally lean meat, as are wild game birds; salmon is an oily fish having its own particular health-giving properties; Christmas cake, plum pudding and mince pies are rich in dried fruit which are high in fibre; and small oranges like satsumas and tangerines give a valuable boost to Vitamin C intakes during winter. The basic goodness of these foods can of course be compromized with such fatty additions as sausage-meat stuffing and suet. Fortunately, there are ways of making more healthy versions of these traditional Christmas foods (recipes for some are given below). You can even make brandy butter using half polyunsaturate margarine. This not only keeps the special flavour but is also much easier to make with a soft margarine!

Balancing Christmas meals

Not everyone wants to eat heavy meals at Christmas and there will be more room for a large dinner if the other meal of the day is kept simple, consisting of a light broth like consommé, or a fresh-tasing soup like carrot, with a treat food like smoked salmon, Parma ham and some good-quality cheese.

Alcohol

As far as adults are concerned the biggest problem at Christmas is usually alcohol. Drinking alcohol

---

recipes

FESTIVE NUT ROAST

Makes a 900 g (2 lb) loaf
1 teaspoon oil
1 large onion, peeled and finely chopped
110 g (4 oz) wholemeal breadcrumbs
60 g (2 oz) each chopped cashew nuts, hazelnuts and peanuts
60 g (2 oz) sunflower seeds
1 medium apple, grated
1 medium carrot, grated
1 teaspoon thyme
1 teaspoon rosemary
1 clove garlic, crushed
110 g (4 oz) mushrooms, sliced
½ red pepper, chopped
½ green pepper, chopped
1 teaspoon yeast extract
1 tablespoon tomato purée
110 ml (4 fl oz) hot water
freshly ground black pepper

Heat the oil in a non-stick frying pan, add the onion and lightly sauté it. Mix the breadcrumbs with the nuts, seeds, apple, carrot and herbs. Add the onion, garlic, mushrooms and peppers.

Dissolve the yeast extract and tomato purée in the water and add sufficient to the nut mixture to form a moist consistency. Season with pepper.

Pile the mixture into a greased and lined 1 kg (2 lb) loaf tin. Bake in a preheated fairly hot oven, 200°C (400°F), Gas Mark 6, for 45 to 60 minutes or until it feels firm to the touch. Serve the nut roast hot or cold.

PRUNE STUFFING

Use this to stuff the neck end of a 6.75 kg (15 lb) turkey. (The body cavity of poultry should never be stuffed because of the risk of food poisoning: see Poultry, page 56.)

Makes 450 g (1 lb)
225 g (8 oz) pitted prunes, chopped
2 slices lemon
cold tea, to cover (see Method)
liver from the turkey
2 pinches nutmeg
225 g (8 oz) fresh breadcrumbs
freshly ground black pepper

Place the prunes in a saucepan with the lemon slices, and cover with tea. Bring to the boil, reduce the heat and simmer for about 10 minutes. Place the turkey liver in a saucepan, cover with water and simmer for 5 minutes.

Drain the liver, reserving the juice, and chop well. Then briefly process in a blender along with the prunes and nutmeg or chop together finely by hand.

Add the breadcrumbs. If the mixture is too crumbly add some of the liquid the liver was cooked in. Season with pepper.

CHRISTMAS FAMILY FRUITCAKE

This looks rich but is much lighter than a normal Christmas cake, as well as being an excellent source of fibre.

Makes one 20 cm (8 inch) cake
340 g (12 oz) mixed fruit
140 g (5 oz) glace cherries, chopped
60 g (2 oz) mixed peel *or* the chopped rind of 1 fresh lemon and 1 orange
60 g (2 oz) walnuts
170 g (6 oz) brown sugar
110 g (4 oz) margarine
1 teaspoon mixed spice
½ teaspoon bicarbonate of soda
275 ml (½ pint) milk
340 g (12 oz) wholemeal self-raising flour
2 × size 3 eggs, beaten

Place all the ingredients except the flour and eggs in a saucepan and bring to the boil. Reduce the heat, stir and simmer the mixture for 5 minutes.

Allow the mixture to cool to blood heat (37°C), then stir in the flour and eggs. Pour into a lined 20 cm (8 inch) cake tin. Wrap the tin in brown paper to prevent the outside of the cake burning. Bake in a preheated moderate oven 160°C (325°F), Gas Mark 3, for 40 minutes. Then reduce the heat to 150° (300°F), Gas Mark 2, and bake for a further 1½ hours.

Allow the fruitcake to cool in the tin.

causes dehydration, which more alcohol merely aggravates rather than reduces. So, if you also have plenty of mineral or iced soda water on hand, you and your guests will be able to dilute their wine into spritzes or simply quench a thirst with a refreshing glass or two of plain water. Drinking plenty of water also helps to avoid hangovers!

Right: a delicious Christmas meal — roast turkey with Festive Nut Roast, Brussels sprouts, potatoes with almonds, roast parsnips and Prune Stuffing, with mince pies to follow

MINCEMEAT

This mincemeat is easy to make, is less fatty than the traditional recipe and tastes much fruitier and less acidic than ready-made varieties.

Makes 1.75 kg (3½ lb)
225 g (8 oz) raisins
225 g (8 oz) sultanas
225 g (8 oz) currants
225 g (8 oz) brown sugar
60 g (2 oz) flaked almonds
85 g (3 oz) candied peel
340 g (12 oz) eating apples, washed, cored and chopped
½ teaspoon cinnamon
¼ teaspoon nutmeg
rind and juice 1 lemon
1 glass sherry *or* brandy
140 ml (5 fl oz) polyunsaturate oil

Place all the ingredients in a large bowl and mix together thoroughly. Turn into a plastic container with a lid, and refrigerate. Leave for a few hours before using. The apple will shrivel a bit during prolonged storage and you may wish to add some more later on.

Store any leftover mincemeat in the fridge or freezer. Stir again thoroughly every time you use some as the liquids will sink to the bottom. This will keep for several days in the fridge, several months in the freezer.

Index

Index

Acknowledgments

The author would like to thank the many friends and family who gave their favourite family recipes and shared their personal experiences, in particular: Catalina Brook, Caroline Burnard, Anona Duncan, Penny Hayes, Liz Illman, Olivia Loewendahl, Ann Morse, Clair Morse, Jane Peirson Jones, Sue Smith and Sue Wells. I would also like to thank Alex, Alexandra, Christopher, Daniel, David, David, Harry, Hugo, Mark, Matthew, Nicholas, Paul, Rory, Rose, Sophie, Timothy, Tom and William who helped taste the recipes. Finally, I am most grateful to Jean James, who has a special expertise in healthy cooking, for her comments.

Conran Octopus would like to thank the following for their help in the preparation of this book:

All the children — and their parents — who took part in the photography: David Bates, Charlotte Bradshaw, Jack Burnham, Charlotte Craig, Peter Cross, Robert Gordon with Joe and Katie, Shuntaro Hara, Henry Johnson, Emily and Madeleine O'Shea, Shama Patel, Guy Taylor, Jessica Walton. For additional artwork: John Hutchinson. For design help: Peter Cross. For their kind permission to reproduce photographs: page 9, John Garratt/Bubbles; page 19, Timothy Woodcock.